Jump into Science

Jump into Science

Themed Science Fairs

Written and Illustrated by Carol Peterson

Teacher Ideas Press

An imprint of Libraries Unlimited
Westport, Connecticut • London

Library of Congress Cataloging-in-Publication Data

Peterson, Carol, 1953–
    Jump into science : themed science fairs / Carol Peterson.
      p. cm.
      Includes bibliographical references and index.
      ISBN-13: 978–1–59158–413–1 (pbk. : alk. paper)
      1. Science projects—Juvenile literature. 2. Science—Experiments—Juvenile literature. I. Title.
    Q182.3.P478 2007
      507.8—dc22   2006037830

British Library Cataloguing in Publication Data is available.

Library of Congress Catalog Card Number: 2006037830
ISBN: 978–1–59158–413–1

First published in 2007

Libraries Unlimited/Teacher Ideas Press, 88 Post Road West, Westport, CT 06881
A Member of the Greenwood Publishing Group, Inc.
www.lu.com

Printed in the United States of America

The paper used in this book complies with the
Permanent Paper Standard issued by the National
Information Standards Organization (Z39.48–1984).

10 9 8 7 6 5 4 3 2 1

This book is dedicated to hubby Jim and my great kids, Doug and Nicole, who share this universe with me and make my life a journey of joy and discovery.

Contents

ECOLOGY UNIT

LIFE SCIENCE UNIT

PHYSICAL SCIENCE UNIT

Introduction

California science standards call it "investigation and experimentation." Missouri's "show-me" standards prefer the "process of scientific inquiry." For Delaware, it's "observation and testing." Regardless of how a state refers to it, curriculum standards are consistent. They require that students know and understand the scientific method—observing, hypothesizing, experimenting, recording, and reporting what they learn. One of the best ways to accomplish this curriculum requirement is through the venue of science fairs. But this does not require an elaborate affair. A simple classroom science fair in which students work individually, in pairs, or as groups and present what they have learned using the scientific method, can help teachers maintain accountability with curriculum standards.

In addition to the scientific method, curriculum standards also seek to ensure that students have a basic understanding of individual areas of science. Although standards vary from state to state as to which grade may cover a particular area of science, they eventually cover the same material. By specifying science fairs by area of science—for example, having a "Life Sciences Science Fair," teachers can present curriculum-specific science, making them further accountable to state standards. Teachers can also maintain tighter control over the focus of experiments, thus avoiding a classroom science fair featuring 23 experiments of begonias grown to music.

Jump into Science is divided into four thematic units; one for each of four themed science fairs. This structure allows teachers to use each unit during the class study of that area of science. Because state standards vary the content of science among grade levels, all experiments are for a general range of grades 4 through 6. The four units are as follows:

Earth Science: Experiments in this unit cover magnetism, rocks and minerals, water and air, and space and Earth's place in it.

Ecology: Experiments in this unit cover exploring ecosystems, understanding our resources, preserving our resources, and our world at risk.

Life Science: Experiments in this unit cover organisms, insects, and animals, plants, and humans.

Physical Science: Experiments in this unit cover chemistry, simple machines, physical forces, and behavior of physical laws.

Jump into Science provides illustrated instructions and checklists for 120 experiments—enough for each child in a classroom of 30 to present his or her own individual project. Simple icons cross-reference other units that an experiment may be used for. This cross-referencing allows greater flexibility and accommodates classes with more than 30 students. The icons are as follows:

Earth Science   Ecology   Life Science   Physical Science

By following the icons, teachers can locate experiments from one themed science unit for use in a different unit. For example, a solar energy experiment in the ecology unit could be used as an experiment when studying physical or earth sciences.

To structure a classroom science fair, teachers choose one of the four themes and assign one project to each student. Students complete their projects and prepare their observations and presentations. The following reproducibles will help both students and teachers have a successful science fair:

- 120 experiments with illustrations when needed

- Tips for students, including guidelines for planning, visual aids, and reports

- Explanation of the scientific method

- Safety rules

- Tips for teachers

- Award certificate

Students will be reading portions of *Jump into Science*. Therefore, experiments are written in grade-appropriate language. Before beginning preparation for the science fair, students should review and understand the scientific method and should be encouraged to follow that method during the experimentation, reporting, and presentation process. A simplified summary of the scientific process, written for students, is provided in the reproducibles at the end of this book. Of course, teachers should first refer to their individual curriculum standards.

Jump into Science also gives teachers the flexibility of doing experiments collectively in the classroom one experiment at a time. Students can also use the experiments for science fairs that are general in nature. However it is used, as a theme-structured resource, *Jump into Science* will help busy teachers address their accountability to required state curriculum science standards in a way that is fun for kids.

Now, get ready. Get set. Let's *Jump into Science*!

EARTH SCIENCE UNIT

Magnetism

Rocks and Minerals

Water and Air

Space and Earth's Place in It

MAGNETISM

Jar and Bar Magnets

Hypothesis or Statement of Purpose: To understand how magnetic fields appear.

What you need:

A wide jar with lid	About 3 tablespoons iron filings
Mineral oil	2 bar magnets

Test, watch, and record: (If you cannot buy iron filings, make them by snipping plain steel wool with scissors. Keep filings away from your eyes.) Fill jar almost completely with oil. Add filings. Slowly add more oil until no air is left in the jar. Screw on the lid and shake the jar. Set jar on flat surface. Place a bar magnet against opposite sides of the jar. Then turn the magnets so the other ends are against the jar. Record your observations.

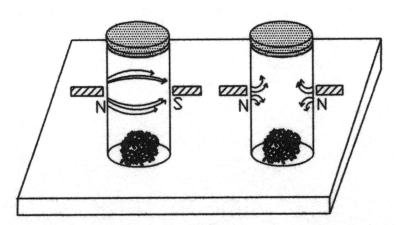

Conclusion/What is going on? Scientists think every atom has a north and south pole. If atoms within a material are jumbled, then the poles of nearby atoms cancel each other, and we are not able to notice its magnetic force. In magnets, the poles of most of the atoms are lined up so the force of the poles is noticed. Shaking the jar distributes the filings in the oil. When magnets are placed against the jar, filings are either attracted or repulsed by the magnets' poles.

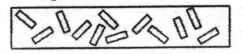

Report and Present: Write out the steps of this experiment and what you saw. Explain the results using "What is going on?" above to help you. Draw what you observed when you flipped the magnets. Display the drawing, the jar and magnets.

From Carol Peterson, *Jump into Science: Themed Science Fairs*. Westport, CT: Teacher Ideas Press. © 2007 by Carol Peterson.

Earth's Magnetic Field

Hypothesis or Statement of Purpose: To understand the shape of the earth's magnetic field.

What you need:

6-inch circle pattern	Paperclip
Sheet of 9-inch by 12-inch construction paper	Spray bottle
Marking pen (color other than black)	White vinegar
Bar magnet	Optional colored marking pens, pencils, or
Iron filings	crayons

Test, watch, and record: (If you cannot buy iron filings, make them by snipping plain steel wool with scissors. Keep the filings away from your eyes.) Touch the magnet to the paperclip to see which end of the magnet attracts metal. Mark that end of the magnet (its north pole) with a pen. Place the paper in front of you. Trace a circle on the paper to represent Earth. Mark Earth's North Pole at the top of the paper and South Pole at the bottom. Fold two sides of the paper about 1 inch from the edge to form a table. Place the magnet under the paper table with its north pole lined up with the North Pole on your paper. Sprinkle the paper with iron filings. Fill a spray bottle with vinegar. Adjust the nozzle to spray a mist. Hold the bottle about 6 inches from the map and spray carefully so you don't scatter the filings. Let dry overnight. Shake filings into the trash.

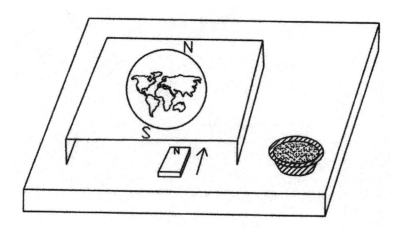

Conclusion/What is going on? The vinegar causes the filings to rust, leaving marks on the paper. The poles of the atoms of the filings are either attracted or repelled by the nearest magnet pole. This turns each filing into a tiny magnet. The north pole of one filing is then attracted to the south pole of the nearest filing, forming curved lines around the bar magnet, called "lines of force." Earth's magnetic field wraps around the Earth from North to South Pole in the same way.

Report and Present: Write out the steps you used in this experiment and what you saw. Explain the results using "What is going on?" to help you. You may take photographs during your experiment and display them, your "Earth" and the magnet.

Hypothesis or Statement of Purpose: To understand properties of magnetic materials.

What you need:

Magnet	Dime
Paperclip	Copper wire
Scissors	Nail
Penny	Other metal items

Test, watch, and record: Hypothesize whether each object is magnetic. Then test by touching the magnet to it. If you can feel the magnetic pull, record the object as magnetic. Compare your results with your hypotheses. Record your observations on a data chart listing:

Name of item:

Hypothesis: (Magnetic/Not Magnetic)

Result: (Attracted/Not Attracted/Not Sure)

Conclusion/What is going on? Scientists think every atom has a north and south pole. If atoms within a material are jumbled, then the poles of nearby atoms cancel each other and we are not able to notice its magnetic force. In magnets, the poles of most of the atoms are lined up so the force of the poles is noticed.

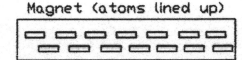

Report and Present: Write out the steps you used and what you saw. Explain the results using "What is going on?" above to help you. Display your chart, the items, and the magnet, and let other students test the magnetic properties of the objects.

From Carol Peterson, *Jump into Science: Themed Science Fairs*. Westport, CT: Teacher Ideas Press.
© 2007 by Carol Peterson.

Magnetic Compass

Hypothesis or Statement of Purpose: To understand magnetic fields of a compass.

What you need:

Stick for stirring	Bar magnet
4 teaspoons plaster of Paris	Sheet of paper
2 teaspoons of water	Marking pen
Paper cup	Paperclip
½ teaspoon iron filings	Compass

Test, watch, and record: Mix the plaster, iron filings, and water in the cup with the stick. Find the magnet's north pole by seeing which end attracts the paperclip. Mark that end of the magnet. Set the magnet on a table and place the cup on top of the north end of the magnet. Let the plaster harden. Place the paper on a nonmetal flat surface and remove the magnet from the area you are working. Turn the cup upside down on a paper. Place the compass on the cup's bottom, which is now on top. Mark a line on the cup about 1 inch up from the surface and a line on the paper at the same point. This is your starting point. Observe the compass needle. When it stops moving, note which direction it went and which direction it is now pointing. Turn the cup to the right one-quarter of the way. Record the direction of the compass needle. Repeat, turning the cup one-quarter of the way each time until you reach the beginning mark. Record your observations.

Cup of plaster and filings on magnet

Conclusion/What is going on? The needle points in a different direction when the cup is turned. A compass needle is a magnet that lines up generally with the Earth's magnetic force. Placing the cup on a magnet turned the filings into tiny magnets—each with its own north and south magnetic poles. The plaster then locked them in place. As you rotated the cup, the poles of the filings also rotated. The compass needle tried to line up with the very close magnetic field of the filings instead of the magnetic field of the Earth that is farther away. Each time the cup (and magnetic filings) turned, the compass needle had to realign.

Report and Present: Write out the steps you took and what you saw. Explain the results using "What is going on?" above to help you. Display the cup, the magnet, and the compass.

Hypothesis or Statement of Purpose: To understand how a compass works by creating one.

What you need:

Magnet	Pencil
Steel needle	Drinking glass
Thread	Paper 1 inch by 2 inches.

Test, watch, and record: Fold the paper in half to make a 1-inch square. Thread a needle and tie the end of the thread in a knot. Push the needle up through the inside of the paper but stop before the knot goes through. Cut the thread next to the needle to remove the needle. Tie the thread to the center of the pencil. Rest the pencil on the rim of the glass and adjust the thread so that the paper hangs 1 inch above the bottom of the glass. Rub the needle in one direction against the magnet 20 times and then insert the needle through both sides of the paper. Center it for balance. Let the needle and paper hang inside the glass. Record your observations.

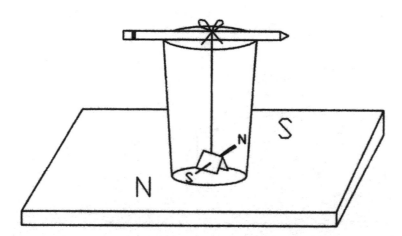

Conclusion/What is going on? Rubbing the needle against the magnet aligned the atoms inside the needle for a short time and turned it into a magnet. Earth has a magnetic North Pole to which the magnet is pulled. Because opposite poles of magnetic fields are attracted to each other, the south pole of the magnetic needle is attracted to the Earth's North Pole as it is in a compass.

Report and Present: Write out the steps and what you observed. Explain the results, using "What is going on?" above to help you. Display your cup and compass. Remagnetize the needle, if needed, by rubbing it against the magnet.

ROCKS AND MINERALS

 ## Earth Metals

Hypothesis or Statement of Purpose: To see whether metals are found in soil.

What you need:

Magnet

Zippered plastic sandwich bag

Magnifying glass

Jar

Water

About ½ cup garden soil

Spoon

Paper towels

Plastic knife

Test, watch, and record: Place the magnet inside the plastic bag and close it. Fill a jar about ¾ full of water. Add the soil and stir quickly. As the water is moving, dip the magnet (in the bag) into the water several times. Lift the bag out of the jar. Open the bag over a paper towel and remove the magnet. With the knife, scrape the particles from the bag onto the towel. Observe them through a magnifying glass.

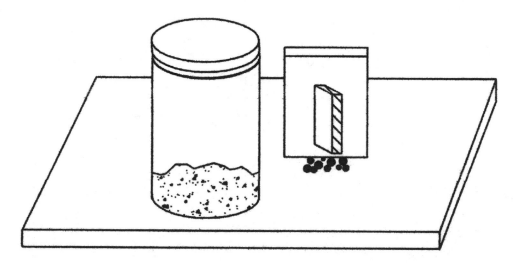

Conclusion/What is going on? Some of the soil stuck to the magnet because they are magnetic particles, called "ferrites."

Report and Present: Write out the steps and what you saw. Explain the results using "What is going on?" above to help you. Describe the particles you observed through the magnifying glass. Make a drawing of one or more of them. Display the particles on a white towel with a magnifying glass, along with your drawings, and the jar of soil and water.

Oxidation

Hypothesis or Statement of Purpose: To understand how oxygen reacts with earth metals.

What you need:

Steel wool (without soap)
Plastic dish
Water
Rubber gloves or plastic bag

Strip of iron or steel (NOT galvanized or stainless steel)
Petroleum jelly
Small piece of wood

Test, watch, and record: Run the steel wool under water and place it in the dish. Clean and dry the iron strip. Coat half of the strip with petroleum jelly on all sides. Dip the iron strip in water and balance it on the wood. Let the steel wool and the strip sit for 7 days. Then cover your hand with a plastic bag or gloves. Crunch the steel wool in your hand. Record your observations about both sets of steel.

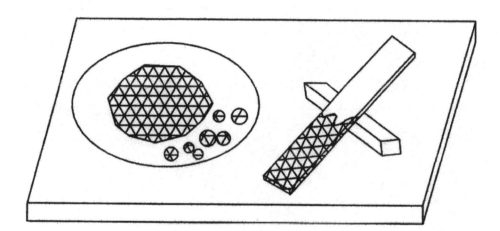

Conclusion/What is going on? Oxygen in the water combines with iron to form oxide, which we call "rust." Rust crumbles easily. The iron on the strip of metal, however, is protected by the petroleum jelly. Oxide is neither the metal nor oxygen, but a new substance.

Report and Present: Write out the steps and what you observed. Explain the results, using "What is going on?" above to help you. Display the rusted steel wool and iron strip.

Hypothesis or Statement of Purpose: To understand how fossils are formed.

What you need:

Modeling clay	Water
Petroleum jelly	Cup
Seashell	Spoon
Plaster of Paris	

Test, watch, and record: Divide clay into two pieces. Flatten each piece until it is larger than the shell. Spread petroleum jelly over the top of each piece of clay. Press the outside of the shell deeply into the clay. Remove the shell and repeat with the second piece of clay. Mix enough plaster of Paris according to the directions to fill the holes. Pour into the holes and let dry.

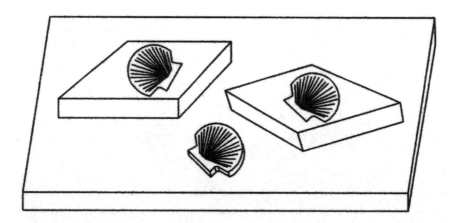

Conclusion/What is going on? The shell leaves an imprint of itself in the clay. A fossil is a record of life that no longer exists. This life is sometimes preserved in soft soil that hardened into rock. The imprint it leaves after it has deteriorated is called a "fossil mold." The fossil mold can be used to show what the original organism looked like. By placing both sides of the plaster shell together, it forms a solid reproduction, called a "cast."

Report and Present: Write out the steps and what you observed. Explain the results, using "What is going on?" above to help you. Display the shell, the two clay molds, and the final cast.

Growing Crystals

Hypothesis or Statement of Purpose: To understand how salt crystals form.

What you need:

Cookie sheet
Sheet of black construction paper
Salt
Warm water

Measuring cup
Tablespoon measurer
Magnifying glass

Test, watch, and record: Place the paper on the cookie sheet. In measuring cup, stir 2 tablespoons of salt into ¼ cup of warm water until dissolved. Pour the salt water over the paper and set it in a sunny place for several days. Observe the paper daily until it is dry. Then observe through a magnifying glass.

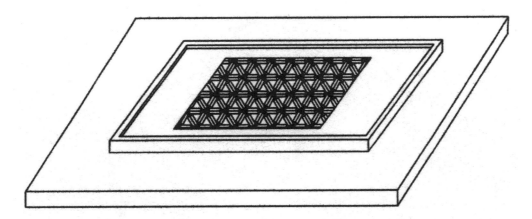

Conclusion/What is going on? At first a layer of white crystals forms. As the water evaporates, separate, white crystals form from the salt.

Report and Present: Write out the steps and what you saw. Explain the results using "What is going on?" above to help you. Draw the crystals you observed. Display your drawings, the crystal-covered paper, and the magnifying glass.

From Carol Peterson, *Jump into Science: Themed Science Fairs*. Westport, CT: Teacher Ideas Press. © 2007 by Carol Peterson.

Stone Splitting

Hypothesis or Statement of Purpose: To understand how ice could affect the Earth's surface.

What you need:

Plastic bowl with lid   Cake pan
Water   Freezer

Test, watch, and record: Fill the plastic bowl completely with water and attach the lid. Set the bowl inside a cake pan to prevent spills and place it in the freezer overnight. When the water is frozen solid, record your observations.

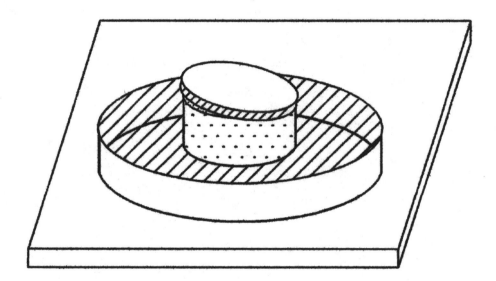

Conclusion/What is going on? When most liquids become solid, their molecules pack tighter together. Atoms that make up water are bonded to each other, so when water freezes, it expands. Because there was no more room inside the bowl, the expanded ice forced the lid off. In nature, water around rocks can freeze and cause rocks to break apart.

Report and Present: Write out the steps and what you saw. Explain the results using "What is going on?" above to help you. Take a photograph or make a drawing of each step of your experiment and include them as part of your presentation.

Natural Bridge

Hypothesis or Statement of Purpose: To understand how natural bridges are formed.

What you need:

Two tables the same height   15 or 20 identical books

Test, watch, and record: Set two tables about 12 inches apart. Place one book on each table so that the edges of the book are even with the inside table edges. Stack books on top of each other, extending each book slightly beyond the edge of the book beneath it, until the top book completes a bridge. Experiment to see how far out can you place a book before it no longer supports the one above. What happens if the first book extends beyond the table edge?

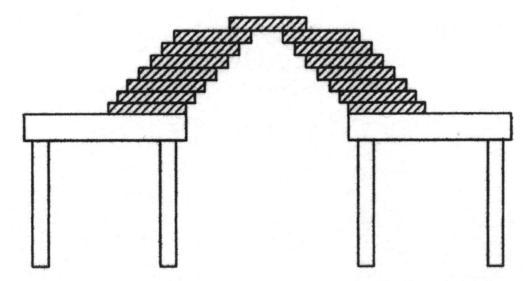

Conclusion/What is going on? Every object has a center of gravity—the point at which the weight on either side of it is equal. Here, the bridge is supported on each side by the center of gravity of the table. In nature, weather and erosion can build up soil and rocks in an overlapping way that places its center of gravity over the rock sides and forms a bridge.

Report and Present: Write out the steps and what you saw. Explain the results using "What is going on?" above to help you. Find a photograph of a natural rock bridge. Display it, along with a drawing showing how your bridge was built.

From Carol Peterson, *Jump into Science: Themed Science Fairs*. Westport, CT: Teacher Ideas Press. © 2007 by Carol Peterson.

P-Waves

Hypothesis or Statement of Purpose: To understand how P-waves (primary pressure waves) travel through the Earth during earthquakes.

What you need:

Five marbles the same size	Duct tape
String	Scissors
Ruler	Table

Test, watch, and record: Cut five pieces of string about 12 inches long. Tape one string securely to each marble. Tape the other end of each string to the edge of a table, so the marbles are at the same height and touch each other. Raise one end marble about 3 inches to the side and release it so it swings back and hits the marble next to it. Record your observations.

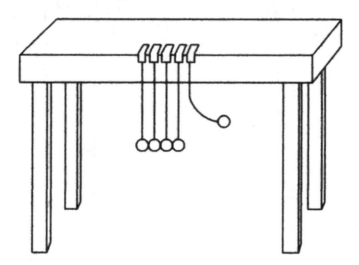

Conclusion/What is going on? The marble hits the marble closest to it and then stops. The marble at the other end of the row swings outward. Then it returns to its starting place and hits the marble next to it. This swinging and hitting continues for a few moments. Lifting the marble gives it energy, which is passed from one marble to the next until the end marble is pushed away. The energy continues to be transferred back and forth until it is used up. This is similar to a P-wave (primary pressure wave) in an earthquake. As the wave moves underneath the Earth's surface, it transfers the energy to nearby particles. Then the particles return to their original position as the energy wave moves on.

Report and Present: Write out the steps and what you observed. Explain the results, using "What is going on?" above to help you. Recreate your experiment.

Recording Earthquakes

Hypothesis or Statement of Purpose: To understand how seismographs record earthquakes.

What you need:

Cardboard box (about 12 inches square and 12 inches high)
Scissors
Adding machine paper
Pencil
Ruler

String
Black marking pen
Masking tape
5-ounce paper cup
Small rocks
Sharp nail

Test, watch, and record: Cut off the top of the box. Place the box on a table with the opening toward you. Cut a circle on the top about 2 inches wide. Cut two slits near the bottom center of the box about 4 inches long and ½ inch wide. Thread the paper through one slit, across the inside of the box and out the second slit.

With a nail, punch one hole in the bottom of the cup and two holes on opposite sides. Cut two pieces of string 18 inches long. Tie one string to each side hole. Then tie the two strings together to form a bucket. Slide the loop up through the hole in the box. Slip a pencil through the loop and tape the string to it. Rest the pencil on the box. Remove the cap from a marking pen and insert the tip of the pen through the bottom cup hole pointing down. Fill the cup with rocks. Turn the pencil to wind the string and raise the cup until the pen just touches the paper. Tape the string to the pencil again so the string will not unwind. Now shake the box. At the same time, pull the paper toward you with the other hand. Observe the marks made by the pen. Try this experiment several times, shaking harder, softer, and longer.

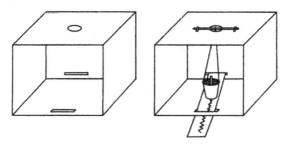

Conclusion/What is going on? A seismograph measures the movement of the Earth's crust (the rock beneath the surface) during an earthquake. Your box shows movement. Your cup, held steady by the rocks, is like a hanging object on a seismograph that remains steady during an earthquake. The pen records the shaking on a moving paper. The width of the marks shows the amount of shaking, called the earthquake's "magnitude."

Report and Present: Write out the steps and what you saw. Explain the results using "What is going on?" above to help you. Display your box and papers. Explain the relationship between the shaking and the width of the marks.

From Carol Peterson, *Jump into Science: Themed Science Fairs.* Westport, CT: Teacher Ideas Press.
© 2007 by Carol Peterson.

Plasticity

Hypothesis or Statement of Purpose: To understand the Earth's mantle.

What you need:

1 cup liquid measuring cup	10 tablespoons cornstarch
Water	Spoon
Large plastic glass	Bowl
Tablespoon measure	

Test, watch, and record: Pour ¼ cup of water into the glass. Stir in 1 tablespoon of cornstarch. Continue to stir in cornstarch, 1 tablespoon at a time. The mixture will become difficult to stir. Tip the glass so half of the mixture flows into the bowl. Observe the flow. Then use the spoon to scrape the remaining mixture into the bowl. Observe how it acts when forced to move. Then rest the spoon against the mixture and allow the spoon to slide through it. Slowly remove the spoon. Repeat, this time lifting the spoon quickly. Record your observations.

Conclusion/What is going on? When the mixture is allowed to flow, it acts like a liquid. When it is forced, it breaks like a solid. Earth is made up of three layers: a thin outer covering called the "crust," the "mantle" just below the crust, and the "core." Scientists believe the core acts like putty—it flows easily if moved slowly (like a liquid) but breaks if it is forced (like a solid). The ability of a solid material to flow is called "plasticity."

Report and Present: Write out the steps and what you observed. Explain the results using "What is going on?" above to help you. Think about the Earth's core and volcanic eruptions. Demonstrate plasticity and allow other students to try this experiment. Have water on hand in case the putty dries during your presentation.

WATER AND AIR

   Water Surface Tension

Hypothesis or Statement of Purpose: To understand how water molecules act.

What you need:

Water	Towels
Pencil	Plastic sheet or garbage bag
Two cups	Rubbing alcohol
Small paperclips	

Test, watch, and record: Cover your work areas with plastic. Place a cup on a level table and fill it to the top with water. Using a second cup, slowly add more water to the first cup until the water is above the rim. Gently drop paperclips into the water, one at a time, end first, until the water spills out. Count and record how many paperclips you can add before it spills out of the cup.

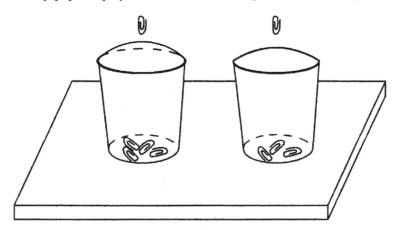

Place a second cup next to the first and fill it with rubbing alcohol. Add alcohol until it is above the rim of the cup. Stand so the cups are at eye level. Compare how high the water and the alcohol are. Gently drop paperclips into the cup of alcohol. Count and record the number of paperclips you can add before the alcohol spills. Compare the two sets of numbers.

Conclusion/What is going on? Water molecules are attracted to each other. That keeps the water together even after it rises above the rim. Finally, the amount of water above the rim is so great that the molecules can no longer hold together. Alcohol molecules have less attraction. So they do not hold together as long and the level of alcohol above the rim of the cup is lower.

Report and Present: Write out the steps and what you saw. Explain the results using "What is going on?" above to help you. Display your glass, water, and paperclips for other students to try the experiment themselves. Set the glass on a small tray and have a towel for spills.

From Carol Peterson, *Jump into Science: Themed Science Fairs*. Westport, CT: Teacher Ideas Press. © 2007 by Carol Peterson.

Effect of Depth on Water Pressure

Hypothesis or Statement of Purpose: To understand the effect of depth on water pressure.

What you need:

Sharp nail   Water
Plastic disposable cup   Sink or bucket
Large pitcher

Test, watch, and record: With the nail, punch a hole in one side of the cup about 1 inch from the bottom. Punch a second hole about 2 inches above the bottom hole but slightly to the side. Set the cup on the edge of the sink or on a table with a bucket beneath the cup. Fill the pitcher with water and pour the water into the cup, fast enough so the water level rises above the two holes. Continue to add water to keep the cup filled. Observe the water flowing out the holes.

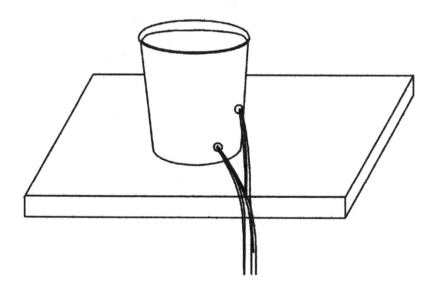

Conclusion/What is going on? Water has weight. The water at the top of the cup pushes down on the water below. Depth affects this pressure. If the water is deeper, there is more weight, and thus the water squirts farther through the bottom hole.

Report and Present: Write out the steps and what you saw. Explain the results using "What is going on?" above to help you. Discuss how this affects SCUBA diving, undersea exploration, and living things at the bottom of the ocean. Make drawings showing the difference of water squirted from the top and bottom holes.

 From Carol Peterson, *Jump into Science: Themed Science Fairs*. Westport, CT: Teacher Ideas Press.

Air Pressure

Hypothesis or Statement of Purpose: To see and hear evidence of air pressure.

What you need:

>Two balloons
>Sharp pin
>Tape measurer

Test, watch, and record: Blow up a balloon with a small amount of air and let the balloon go. Measure and record the distance before it lands. Then fill it with a medium amount of air and release it. Measure and record that distance. Then fill the balloon with as much air as you can and release it. Measure and record that distance. Blow the balloon up again and hold the end tightly. Relax your hold to allow air to escape slowly. Blow the balloon up again and tie the end. Hold the balloon by the tied end and poke it with the pin. Record your observations at each step.

Conclusion/What is going on? The amount of air in the balloon results in more air pressure inside it and causes the air to rush out when it can. This rush of air makes the balloon fly when released, vibrate to make a squealing noise, or make a "bang" when the balloon is stabbed.

Report and Present: Write out the steps and what you saw. Explain the results using "What is going on?" above to help you. Have extra balloons on hand for students to use.

From Carol Peterson, *Jump into Science: Themed Science Fairs.* Westport, CT: Teacher Ideas Press. © 2007 by Carol Peterson.

Atmospheric Pressure

Hypothesis or Statement of Purpose: To understand the effect of atmospheric pressure.

What you need:

Flat dish or cake pan

Large jar without lid

Plastic coffee can cover wider than jar
    opening

Scissors

Two 6-inch long pieces of 1-inch by 1-inch wood

Masking tape

Ruler

Water

Spoon

Test, watch, and record: Using your ruler, measure the width of the jar opening. Tape two pieces of wood to the bottom of the cake pan, that distance apart. Fill the pan with water so the water covers the wood by about 1 inch. Fill the jar with water. Cut the lip from the coffee can lid. Place the coffee can cover over the opening of the jar. Carefully turn the jar over and set it on the wood. Make sure the opening of the jar is completely under water. Slide the cover away from jar. Observe the water level in the jar and the pan. Spoon water from the pan. Record what happens to the water level in the jar.

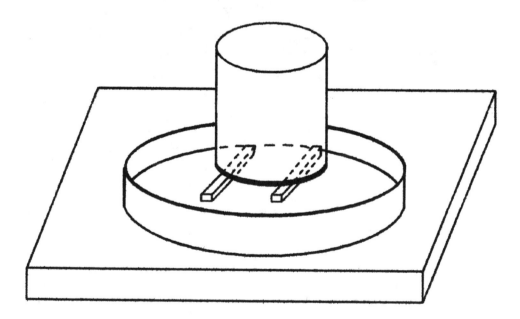

Conclusion/What is going on? The flow of water from the jar into the pan will stop when the water level in the pan reaches the height of the jar opening. The air above us is pulled toward the Earth by gravity. One hundred miles of air above us pushes down on the water in the pan to keep the bottle filled. There is less air inside the jar to push down on that water. So the water level inside is higher. This is how a pet water dish works.

Report and Present: Write out the steps and what you saw. Explain the results using "What is going on?" above to help you. Display your pet water dish.

Aneroid Barometer

Hypothesis or Statement of Purpose: To understand how a barometer works.

What you need:

Tall glass jar with wide mouth	Rubber cement
Round balloon	Several rubber bands
String	Sharp nail
Ruler	Styrofoam sheet about 2 inches thick and 1 foot long by
Thin wire (or drinking straw)	6 or 8 inches wide

Test, watch, and record: Cut a sheet of rubber from a round balloon. Wipe rubber cement around the jar opening. Stretch the rubber over it, securing it with rubber bands. Glue one end of the wire to the center of the rubber with rubber cement. Slice a narrow 2-inch long groove into the center of the Styrofoam with the nail, about 1 inch from one edge. Slide one end of the ruler into the groove so it stands up. Place the jar on top of the Styrofoam so the wire points to the ruler. Record the level of the wire on the ruler over the next several days.

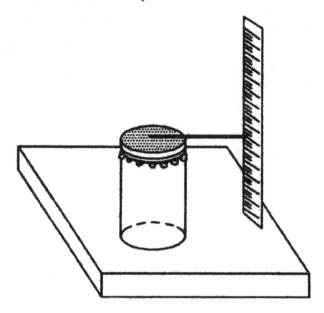

Conclusion/What is going on? A barometer is used to measure air pressure that can hint at what kind of weather may be coming. For example, warm, moist air may bring rain because warm air can rise and form clouds. Dry air is usually heavy and brings clear weather. The wire on your barometer will go up or down to reflect this change in air pressure.

Report and Present: Write out the steps and what you saw. Explain the results using "What is going on?" above to help you. Display your barometer and data table.

From Carol Peterson, *Jump into Science: Themed Science Fairs*. Westport, CT: Teacher Ideas Press. © 2007 by Carol Peterson.

Anemometer

Hypothesis or Statement of Purpose: To understand wind velocity.

What you need:

Five small (3-ounce) paper cups   Ruler
Two plastic soda straws (not bendable)   Clock with second hand
Straight pin   Marking pen
Scissors   Small rock
Stapler   Ruler
Pencil   Electric fan or a windy day
Eraser   Large chunk of modeling clay (if using a fan)
Sharp nail

Test, watch, and record: Label the cups 1, 2, 3, 4, and 5. With a nail, make one hole in cups 1, 2, 3, and 4, about ½ inch down from the rim. On cup 5, punch four holes, about ¼ inch below the rim, spaced equally from each other. Make a hole in the bottom of cup 5.

Slide a straw through the hole of cup 1. Fold the end of the straw flat against the side of the cup opposite to the hole. Staple in place. Repeat with the second straw and cup 2. Slide the free end of the first straw through one of the top holes in cup 5 and on through the hole of cup 3. Make sure the single-hole cups face the same direction. Fold the straw end flat against the side of cup 3, opposite the hole and staple. Repeat with the second straw through cup 5 and into the hole in cup 4. Poke the pencil point around and under the crossed straws and out through the bottom hole of cup 5. Then push the pin through where the two straws cross and into the pencil eraser. With your marker, make a design on cup 1.

Push the pencil into the soil or into a lump of clay in front of an electric fan (set at lowest speed). Place the rock beneath the decorated cup. As the secondhand of the clock passes "12," count the number of times the decorated cup passes the rock. Stop counting when the second hand reaches "12" again. Record that number.

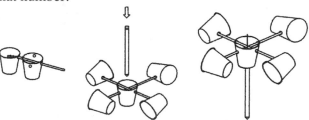

Conclusion/What is going on? Your anemometer will spin in the wind. Your number is the anemometer's "revolutions" per minute (RPM). An accurate anemometer will calculate wind velocity (speed) as one way to understand weather patterns.

Report and Present: Write out the steps and what you saw. Explain the results using "What is going on?" above to help you. Create a data table and do this experiment at different times of the day, on different days, or if using a fan, on different speeds or different distances away. Display your data table and anemometer.

From Carol Peterson, *Jump into Science: Themed Science Fairs*. Westport, CT: Teacher Ideas Press.
© 2007 by Carol Peterson.

SPACE AND EARTH'S PLACE IN IT

Earth's Tilt

Hypothesis or Statement of Purpose: To understand the Earth's tilt.

What you need:

A sharp pencil
A Styrofoam ball about 3 inches in
  diameter

Marking pen
Flashlight

Test, watch, and record: With a marker, draw a circle around the center of the ball. Push a pencil into the bottom. In a dark room, hold the pencil in your left hand at an angle of about 23 degrees tilted to the right (almost the angle between the "12" and the "1" on a clock). Hold the flashlight in your right hand. Shine it toward the ball about 6 inches away. Observe where the light hits the ball (above the line). Now hold the pencil and ball in your right hand at the same angle tilted to the right. Hold the flashlight in your left hand and shine it at the ball about 6 inches away. Observe where the light hits the ball (below the line). Record your observations.

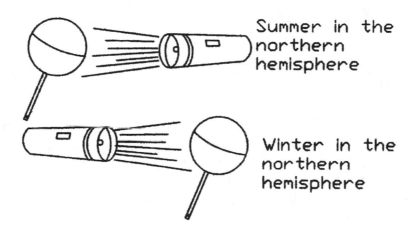

Summer in the
northern
hemisphere

Winter in the
northern
hemisphere

Conclusion/What is going on? The line represents the equator—the point that divides the northern half of the Earth from the southern half. In the first step, the top half of the ball receives the most light from the flashlight. This represents the "summer solstice," around June 21 each year, when the northern half of the Earth gets the most sunshine. The second step shows the "winter solstice," around December 21 each year, when the southern half of Earth gets the most sunshine. The dates in the southern hemisphere are reversed—summer is in December and winter is in June. Halfway between the solstices, the sun hits the equator. Those times are called the spring and fall "equinoxes." The Earth's tilt and change in amount of direct sunlight causes our seasons.

Report and Present: Write out the steps and what you saw. Explain the results using "What is going on?" above to help you. Draw a diagram of the Earth and its position to the sun during different times of the year. Display your diagram and the ball and flashlight.

From Carol Peterson, *Jump into Science: Themed Science Fairs*. Westport, CT: Teacher Ideas Press.
© 2007 by Carol Peterson.

Angle of Descent

Hypothesis or Statement of Purpose: To understand how angle affects the pull of gravity.

What you need:

A paper towel tube

Marble

Two or three books

Test, watch, and record: Lay the tube on a level surface. Release a marble into one end, tipping the tube slightly so that the marble rolls out the other end. Now place one end of the tube on the edge of a stack of books. Release the marble down the tube. Now hold the tube straight up and down (a 90-degree angle). Release the marble. Compare the speed of the marble when the tube is almost flat, when it is on the books, and when it is straight up and down.

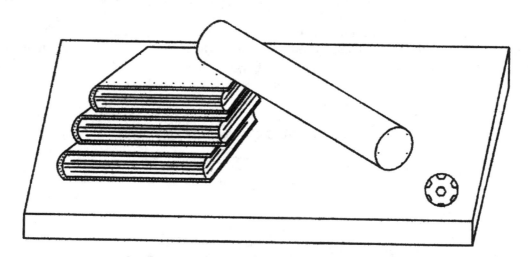

Conclusion/What is going on? Increasing the angle of the tube increases the downward pull of gravity and the marble's velocity (speed). When humans first flew into space, the spacecraft could not fly back to Earth. Rather, astronauts inside the space capsule basically fell back to Earth at a 90-degree angle. Because the Space Shuttle can be flown back to Earth, its descent can be controlled. So it comes in at a much lower, 40-degree angle for an easier landing.

Report and Present: Write out the steps and what you saw. Explain the results using "What is going on?" above to help you. Find photos or create drawings showing how early space capsules descended compared with how the Space Shuttle lands. Display items, diagrams, and drawings.

 From Carol Peterson, *Jump into Science: Themed Science Fairs*. Westport, CT: Teacher Ideas Press. © 2007 by Carol Peterson.

Foucault's Pendulum

Hypothesis or Statement of Purpose: To understand and observe the Earth's rotation.

What you need:

2-liter plastic soda bottle with cap	Scissors
Sand to almost fill bottle	Masking tape
Nylon cord	Funnel
Sharp nail	Large sheet of black paper or several sheets taped together
Hammer	
Piece of wood	Tall ladder

Test, watch, and record: Place the cap on the wood, open side down. Make a small hole in the center of the cap with a hammer and nail. Remove the nail. Cover the hole with masking tape. Punch four holes around the bottom of the bottle with a hammer and nail. Enlarge the holes with a pencil. Cut two 4-foot pieces of cord. Wrap one end of each cord with tape. Thread the cords through two opposite holes and out the other side of the bottle to cross in the center. Tie the ends together. Cover all holes with tape. Using a funnel, fill the bottle almost full of sand. Tie the cords to the center of a folding ladder so the bottle hangs about 3 inches above the ground. Place paper underneath.

Have a friend hold the ladder steady. Walk backward, holding the bottle and keeping the cord tight, until the bottle is waist high. Remove the tape on the cap and release the bottle. As the bottle swings, the sand traces a line on the paper. Keep the bottle swinging for at least 15 minutes by gently pushing it every three or four swings. Make sure not to change its direction.

Conclusion/What is going on? In the Northern Hemisphere, the line of sand shifts to the right because the Earth rotates clockwise. The rate of shift depends on how close you are to the pole or the equator. At the poles, the sand would trace a complete circle. At the equator, it wouldn't shift at all. In the Southern Hemisphere, the line shifts the other way.

Report and Present: Write out the steps and what you saw. Explain the results using "What is going on?" above to help you. This experiment is too large to recreate at a science fair, so make drawings or photos showing the beginning, middle, and end of the experiment.

From Carol Peterson, *Jump into Science: Themed Science Fairs*. Westport, CT: Teacher Ideas Press. © 2007 by Carol Peterson.

Mass and Gravity

Hypothesis or Statement of Purpose: To understand how gravity affects weight and mass.

What you need:

Golf ball	Ping-pong ball
Tennis ball	Feather
Large marble	Two metal cake pans or buckets
1-inch Styrofoam ball	

Test, watch, and record: Stand with a pan or bucket on each side of you. Hold one ball in each hand at the same height. Drop them at the same time, listening for the sound as they hit the metal. Which lands first? Record your observations. Repeat with all balls, then repeat using a feather and a ping-pong ball.

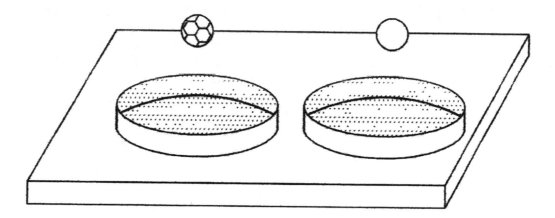

Conclusion/What is going on? You might guess that heavy items would land before lighter ones. But gravity is pulling both toward Earth at the same speed. So even though they weigh different amounts, they land at the same time. The feather and ping-pong ball both weigh about the same. But air pushes up more against the feather than the ping-pong ball, so the ball lands first. In 1971, astronauts dropped a feather and a hammer on the moon at the same time. There is no air on the moon to work against the feather, so they landed at the same time.

Report and Present: Write out the steps and what you saw. Explain the results using "What is going on?" above to help you. Display these items and have other students try this experiment.

From Carol Peterson, *Jump into Science: Themed Science Fairs.* Westport, CT: Teacher Ideas Press. © 2007 by Carol Peterson.

View of the Moon from Earth

Hypothesis or Statement of Purpose: To understand how the moon appears during the month.

What you need:

Shoebox	Sharp nail
2-inch Styrofoam ball	Ruler
Thread	1-inch circle pattern (such as a bottle top)
Paper clip	Black marker
Brass fastener	Scissors
Glue	Flashlight
Yellow construction paper	Books
Pencil	

Test, watch, and record: Remove the lid from the box. With a nail, make eight holes in the sides of the box—one on each end and three on each side. Enlarge the holes with a pencil. With a marker, number the holes inside and outside: the end holes 1 and 5; the holes on one side 2, 3, 4; the holes on the other side 6, 7, 8. With the nail, punch a hole 1-inch below hole 5. Enlarge this hole with scissors to fit a flashlight. With the bottle cap and pencil, trace eight circles on yellow paper and cut out. Draw the moon phases on the circles and color in with the marker. Glue each circle above its matching hole on the outside of the box.

Straighten one end of a paperclip and push it into the ball. Measure from hole 1 to the box top. Cut thread 1 inch longer than the measurement. Loop the thread on the paperclip. Tie the other end to the fastener. Push the fastener into the center of the lid, with the ball hanging from it. Replace the lid. Rest the flashlight on books so it fits through the hole. Turn on the flashlight and look through each hole. Does the moon match the pattern for the hole?

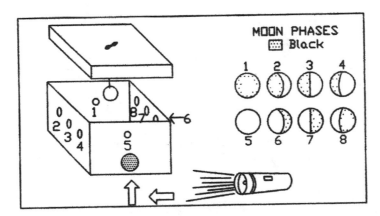

Conclusion/What is going on? This experiment simulates our view of the moon from its different positions in our sky during a lunar month. The flashlight simulates the sun.

Report and Present: Write out the steps and what you saw. Explain the results using "What is going on?" above to help you. Display the box and flashlight.

Hypothesis or Statement of Purpose: To understand how gravity and friction affect meteors.

What you need:

Hammer

Long nail

Block of wood 4 inches by 4 inches by 4 inches or larger

Test, watch, and record: Carefully hammer a nail into the block of wood. After several hits, touch the head of the nail. Record your observations.

Conclusion/What is going on? The head of the nail becomes hot because of friction from pounding the metal hammer against the metal nail. When a meteor comes close to Earth, gravity pulls it into our atmosphere. There the meteor rubs against molecules in the atmosphere. This friction heats the meteor until it is burned up. The light we see as it is burning is called a "shooting star." Every year, Earth passes through the orbits of specific comets. We see these "meteor showers" around January 3, August 12, October 21, and December 14. A meteor that does not burn up completely but reaches the Earth is called a "meteorite."

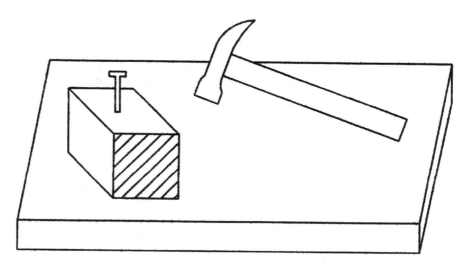

Report and Present: Write out the steps and what you observed. Explain the results using "What is going on?" above to help you. How does this relate to space travel and the need to protect spacecraft? Have your hammer and extra nails so other students can try this. Include a drawing of how meteors might look entering our atmosphere or a photograph of a meteor shower. Find out which comets' orbits the Earth travels through each year.

 From Carol Peterson, *Jump into Science: Themed Science Fairs*. Westport, CT: Teacher Ideas Press.

Effect of Distance on the Orbit Speed of Planets

Hypothesis or Statement of Purpose: To understand how distance from the sun affects planets' orbiting speed.

What you need:

Metal washer   Scissors
Tape measure   String

Test, watch, and record: Using the tape measure and scissors, measure and cut a 3-foot-long piece of string. Tie the metal washer securely to one end of the string. Wrap the other end around one hand. Hold the end of the string out from your body and begin to swing it in a circle close to the floor. Use the least speed you can to keep the washer going in a circle with the string remaining tight. Then hold the string at its middle and swing it in a circle, using the least speed you can to keep the washer going in a circle with the string remaining tight. Then hold the string at about 1 foot from the washer and swing it in a circle, using the least speed you can to keep the washer going in a circle with the string remaining tight. Record your observations.

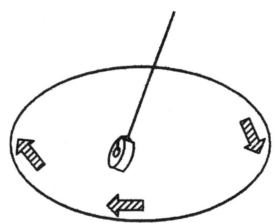

Conclusion/What is going on? The length of the string represents a planet's distance from the sun. The farther the planet is away from the sun, the longer its orbit. Also the farther away from the sun, the less the planet feels the pull of the sun's gravity. Therefore, the planet does not need to spin as fast. Mercury, closest to our sun, has the shortest and fastest orbit. Pluto, farther from the sun, has the longest and slowest orbit.

Report and Present: Write out the steps and what you observed. Explain the results using "What is going on?" above to help you. Think about where Earth is in the solar system and how its orbit compares with Mercury and Pluto. Have someone take photographs as you perform your experiment or make drawings of the steps. Include a drawing, diagram, model, or picture of the solar system to show the relationship between the known planets and our sun.

What Keeps a Satellite in Orbit?

Hypothesis or Statement of Purpose: To understand what keeps a satellite in orbit around a planet.

What you need:

Cookie sheet with sides	Water
Masking tape	Food color
Empty toilet paper tube	Spoon
Cup	Marble
Sheet of 8½ by 11–inch paper	Paper towel

Test, watch, and record: Set the cookie sheet on a table. Tape the tube to the rim of one short side of the cookie sheet. Slide a paper underneath the bottom of the tube. Fill the cup with water and stir in food coloring until water is a dark color. Wet the marble in the colored water and release it through the top of the tube. Observe the path made by the marble across the paper. Now fold a paper towel several times and place it under one corner of the cookie sheet to raise it. Wet and release the marble again and observe its new path. Record your observations.

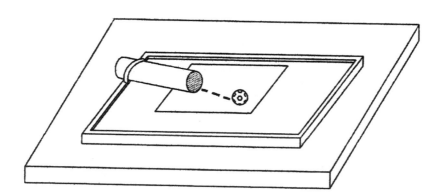

Conclusion/What is going on? On the flat pan, the marble's path will be straight. Gravity pulls the marble down the tube and holds it on the pan in a straight line. On the tilted pan, the marble moves forward as it leaves the tube. Then gravity pulls it downward. The combination of the marble's forward and downward motion results in a curved path. A satellite's curved path is called an "orbit." Without gravity, satellites would keep going straight out into space. Without forward speed, gravity would pull the satellite down to the planet. The two forces work together to keep a satellite in a curved orbit around a planet.

Report and Present: Write out the steps and what you observed. Explain the results using "What is going on?" above to help you. Think about how this experiment relates to the Earth's orbit around the sun; to the Moon's orbit around the Earth; and to satellites' and the Space Station's orbit around Earth. Have the items set up for other students to conduct the experiment. Display your paper showing the paths of the marble.

 From Carol Peterson, *Jump into Science: Themed Science Fairs*. Westport, CT: Teacher Ideas Press. © 2007 by Carol Peterson.

Why Planets Continue to Spin

Hypothesis or Statement of Purpose: To understand the effect of friction and inertia on planets.

What you need:

Pencil   Round cake pan
Scissors   Construction paper (any color)
Marble

Test, watch, and record: Place the pan on the paper and trace around it. Cut out the circle and place it inside the pan. Place the pan on a flat surface and set the marble spinning against the insides. Count and record the number of times the marble rolls completely around the pan before slowing. Remove the paper and roll the marble inside the pan again. Count and record the number of times the marble circles the pan before slowing. Try to make sure you use a similar speed with and without the paper. Try this experiment using paper of different thicknesses, cloth, or sandpaper to change the amount of friction.

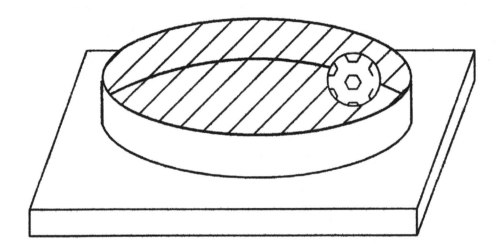

Conclusion/What is going on? The marble rolls faster, smoother, and longer without the paper. "Inertia" is a force that means objects want to keep going the same way they started, or they want to NOT move if they are stopped. "Friction" is a force that acts against objects to make movement difficult. The marble stopped moving sooner in a paper-lined pan because paper added friction. In space, there is no atmosphere to cause friction, so planets continue to spin because of inertia and because they are not slowed by friction.

Report and Present: Write out the steps and what you observed. Explain the results using "What is going on?" above to help you. Have the cake pan, marble, and paper handy for other students to reproduce the experiment.

From Carol Peterson, *Jump into Science: Themed Science Fairs*. Westport, CT: Teacher Ideas Press. © 2007 by Carol Peterson.

Hypothesis or Statement of Purpose: To understand the relationship between friction and conservation of energy and electricity in Jupiter's atmosphere.

What you need:

> Plastic food wrap about 12 inches long
>
> Wool cloth about 12 inches square
>
> A dark room or closet

Test, watch, and record: Rub your hands together slowly for a count of 10. Observe how hot they feel. Pause for a count of 20 to allow your hands to cool. Now rub your hands together quickly for a count of 10. Observe how hot your hands feel. Compare and record your observations. Now go into a dark room. Hold the plastic in a bunch. Wrap the cloth around the plastic and drag the plastic through the cloth quickly several times. Record your observations.

Conclusion/What is going on? The closer and faster objects move, the greater the heat they make. Jupiter's atmosphere is made of gasses that are blown against each other by Jupiter's strong wind, causing friction. In the dark room, you saw flashes of light. Electrons are negative particles, which spin around the nucleus of an atom. The nucleus is positively charged. When the wool is rubbed against the plastic, the electrons from the wool are rubbed onto the plastic, leaving the wool positively charged. An electric spark is created when the electrons jump from the plastic back onto the wool. Winds on Jupiter rub molecules in the atmosphere together in the same way. The result is continuous flashes of lightning.

Report and Present: Write out the steps and what you observed. Explain the results, using "What is going on?" above to help you. Have other students try rubbing their hands together.

ECOLOGY UNIT

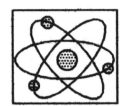

Exploring Ecosystems

Understanding Our Resources

Preserving Our Resources

Our World at Risk

EXPLORING ECOSYSTEMS

 ## Desert Biome

Hypothesis or Statement of Purpose: To understand a desert ecosystem.

What you need:

Fish tank or large clear glass or plastic
  container
Water container
Gravel
Sand

Topsoil
Incandescent light
Very small plants (such as jade; succulents,
  cactus)

Test, watch, and record: Layer 1 inch of gravel on the bottom of the tank. Mix 1 cup topsoil and 5 cups of sand, doubling or tripling the amount if needed to cover the gravel. Spread 2 more inches of sand on top. Make small holes in the sand for the plants. Cover the roots carefully. Sprinkle with enough water to moisten the soil. Sprinkle ½ cup water over the biome each week after that. Set a light over the tank and leave it on for 10 hours a day. Record plant growth and health over several weeks if possible. If you find insects eating the plants, remove them. If they are not eating the plants, keep them in the biome and include them in your observations.

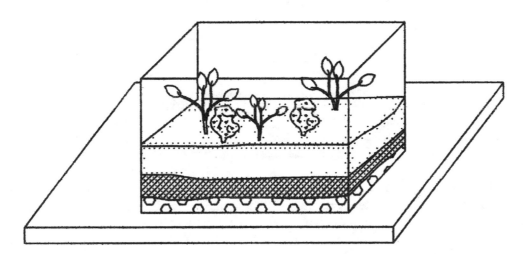

Conclusion/What is going on? A biome contains plants and organisms from a specific environment. The type of soil, water, light, and temperature is similar to that of a desert ecosystem, without the insects and animals found there. By creating a small environment, we can better understand the larger one.

Report and Present: Write out the steps you used in creating this biome. Explain the results using "What is going on?" above to help you. Discuss the plants, soil, and weather required for this biome. Research and report the types of animals that would live in a desert ecosystem. Display the biome.

Garden Biome

Hypothesis or Statement of Purpose: To understand a garden ecosystem.

What you need:

Fish tank or large clear glass or plastic container

Water container

Gravel

Sand

Topsoil

Incandescent light

Very small plants that you would find in a garden

Test, watch, and record: Layer 1 inch of gravel and then 1 inch of sand on the bottom of the tank. Spread 2 inches of topsoil over the sand. Make small holes in the sand for the plants. Cover the roots carefully. Sprinkle with enough water to moisten the soil. Sprinkle a ½ cup of water over the biome each week after that. Set a light over the tank and leave it on 8 hours a day. Record plant growth and health over several weeks, if possible. If you find insects eating the plants, remove them. If they are not eating the plants, keep them in the biome and include them in your observations.

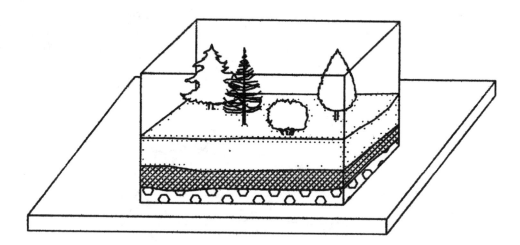

Conclusion/What is going on? A biome contains plants and organisms from a specific environment. The type of soil, water, light, and temperature is similar to that of a garden ecosystem, without the insects and animals often found there. By creating a small environment, we can better understand the larger one.

Report and Present: Write out the steps you used in creating this biome. Explain the results using "What is going on?" above to help you. Discuss the plants, soil, and weather required for this biome. Research and report the types of animals that would live in a garden ecosystem. Display the biome.

From Carol Peterson, *Jump into Science: Themed Science Fairs*. Westport, CT: Teacher Ideas Press.
© 2007 by Carol Peterson.

Forest Biome

Hypothesis or Statement of Purpose: To understand a forest biome.

What you need:

Fish tank or large clear glass or plastic container	Sand
	Topsoil
Water container	Incandescent light
Gravel	Very small plants and trees found in a forest

Test, watch, and record: Layer 1 inch gravel on bottom of tank and 1 inch sand over the gravel. Mix 2 cups of topsoil and 1 cup of sand. Double or triple the amount to cover the sand by 2–3 inches. Make small holes in the sand for the plants. Cover the roots carefully. Sprinkle less than 2 cups of water. Set a light over the tank and leave it on 5 to 6 hours a day. Check daily and keep ¼ inch of water in the gravel. Record plant growth and health in the biome over several weeks, if possible. If mushrooms (fungus) grow, reduce the amount of water you add and remove the mushrooms. Make sure to wash your hands afterward. Record plant growth and health. If you find insects eating the plants, remove them. If they are not eating the plants, keep them in the biome and include them in your observations.

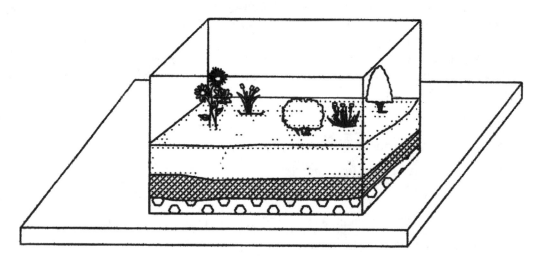

Conclusion/What is going on? A biome contains plants and organisms from a specific environment. The type of soil, water, light, and temperature is similar to that of a forest ecosystem, without the insects and animals often found there. By creating a small environment, we can better understand the larger one.

Report and Present: Write out the steps you used in creating this biome. Explain the results using "What is going on?" above to help you. Discuss the plants, soil, and weather required for this biome. Research and report the types of animals that would live in a forest ecosystem. Display the biome.

Understanding a Garden Ecosystem

Hypothesis or Statement of Purpose: To understand conditions in a garden ecosystem.

What you need:

Measuring tape	Sharp pencil
String	Thermometer
Six to eight large paper clips	Six to eight small zippered plastic bags
Trowel or small shovel	

Test, watch, and record: Using the tape measurer, mark off an area in your garden, field, park, or school 1 foot wide and 1 foot long. Place the string at the boundaries of that section and hold the string in place by unbending one end of the paperclips, hooking the string through them and pushing the straight end of the paperclips into the soil. Observe the area within the string. Record the types of plants located inside, any insects on the surface, and the appearance of the soil, including whether it is wet or dry. Measure and record the height of plants. Take photographs or make drawings of what you see. Stick a pencil into the soil to a depth of 6 inches. Then remove the pencil and slide the thermometer in the hole. Leave it for 5 minutes. Then remove it and record the temperature. Let the thermometer sit on top of the soil, in the center of the area for 5 minutes. Record the surface temperature. If you are permitted to do so, dig underneath the soil and examine what is there. Take a sample of some of the plants, rocks, and soil in the area, placing each sample in a separate zippered bag. Record which plant, rock, or other thing covers most of your area and the area surrounding it. Record signs of animal and insect life. Include evidence of holes or leaves that have been eaten. Record water conditions (recent rainfall, sprinkling system, runoff), time of day, shadiness or sunlight. Create a data table including the following:

Location

Description—sun, shade, level ground, slope, hill

Temperature: surface; underground

Soil: wet, dry, color, sandy, rocky, clay

Plant life: number/description, healthy or dying, coverage by each type; measurements

Animal/insects: types found; evidence of life

Conclusion/What is going on? The 1-foot area is an entire ecosystem. By observing it, you can see the relationship between conditions, plants, and creatures that are part of the ecosystem.

Report and Present: Write out the steps you used and what you saw. Explain the results using "What is going on?" above to help you. Make drawings or take photographs. Display your data chart and any photographs, drawings, or samples you have.

Ant Tunnels

Hypothesis or Statement of Purpose: To understand how ants tunnel.

What you need:

- 2 wide-mouth jars such as mayonnaise jars
- A clean, empty frozen juice can
- Small bowl or jar top, larger around than the can but small enough to fit through the jar opening
- Nylon netting about 12 inches by 12 inches
- Large rubber band
- Sheet of white paper
- About 2 cups garden soil
- Ants
- Garden or work gloves
- Small block of wood about 1 inch high and small enough to fit in the pan
- Aluminum foil pie pan
- Sheet of black paper
- Tape
- Garden trowel or large spoon
- Bread or fruit

Test, watch, and record: Wearing gloves, lift rocks in the garden to locate ants. Collect ants by scooping them and soil with the trowel or spoon. Place the soil and ants onto the white paper. Break up large clumps of soil and remove rocks. Roll the paper and tap the soil and ants into a jar. Cover the jar. Continue to dig in the soil until you find ants and larvae together. You should then find a larger and pale-colored ant. This is the queen. Place her in the jar with the other ants.

Place the juice can inside the second jar and pour the soil and ants into the jar on the outside of the can. Set a small dish on top of the can. Fill the dish with water. Cover the mouth of the jar with netting and tie with a rubber band. Set the wood in the pie tin and rest the jar on the wood. Fill the pie tin with water. Cover the side of the jar with black paper and tape in place. Set the jar on the wood for 24 hours. Remove the black paper cover. Record your observations.

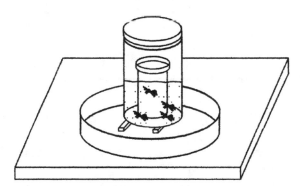

Conclusion/What is going on? The ants have dug new tunnels in the soil. Research classes of ants in a colony and identify the classes you can find: winged, fertile females; wingless infertile females or workers; winged males, soldier. Photograph or draw the ants and label them for your report and presentation.

Report and Present: Write out the steps and what you saw. Explain the results using "What is going on?" above to help you. Display your colony. Sprinkle breadcrumbs or bits of fruit on top of the soil to keep your ants alive.

From Carol Peterson, *Jump into Science: Themed Science Fairs*. Westport, CT: Teacher Ideas Press. © 2007 by Carol Peterson.

Web Masters

Hypothesis or Statement of Purpose: To understand spider webs.

What you need:

Several sheets of black paper

Spray adhesive

Test, watch, and record: You will collect spider webs for this experiment. The best time for collecting is early morning. Some spiders are poisonous, so DO NOT TOUCH THE SPIDER. When you locate a web, hold a piece of black paper against it. Spray adhesive over the web and the paper so the web attaches to it. Record your observations about the location of the web, the time of day, and whether the web contains any insects.

Conclusion/What is going on? Different types of spiders create different shapes of webs. If you are able to see the spider, photograph or draw it. Do not try to catch it because some spiders are poisonous. Try to find out what kind of spider it is. Describe where you found the web—inside the house, outside, or attached to a plant or the house.

Report and Present: Write out the steps and what you saw. Explain the results using "What is going on?" above to help you. Display your webs and any photographs or drawings you have.

UNDERSTANDING OUR RESOURCES

  ## Clock Compass

Hypothesis or Statement of Purpose: To show how a clock can be used as a compass to understand the relationship of places on Earth.

What you need:

Ruler	Straight pin
Pencil or pen	Cardboard about 12 inches square
Magnetic compass	Clock or watch with correct time
6-inch paper plate	

Test, watch, and record: Using the ruler, find the center of the paper plate and draw a line through it to divide the circle in half vertically. Do the same to divide it in half horizontally. Write a "12" at the top of the circle; a "6" at the bottom of the circle; a "3" on the right side; and a "9" on the left side. Fill in the other numbers as if it were a clock. Place the plate on the cardboard and insert the pin in the center, where the two lines meet. Then place both outside in the sun. Turn the circle until the shadow of the pin falls on the correct time. The direction of north will be the halfway point between the shadow and the 12 on the plate. Use a magnetic compass to check your observations.

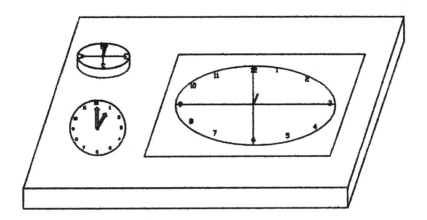

Conclusion/What is going on? This compass is most accurate on the spring and fall equinoxes when the shadow points north near noontime. It is not as accurate at other times of the year but can still be used to find the general direction of north. Check the sun's location in the sky. Earth moves around the sun, but from our place on Earth, the sun appears to make a path across the sky from east to west. How could you determine direction, knowing that the sun is generally directly overhead at noon?

Report and Present: Write out the steps and what you saw. Explain the results using "What is going on?" above to help you. Present how you might use this clock compass if you were lost or needed to know the general direction of someplace you were going. Display the compass clock.

Comparing Trees

Hypothesis or Statement of Purpose: To understand our environment by observing differences in types of trees.

What you need:

Tape measurer

Several sheets of paper

Crayons

Test, watch, and record: Locate several different types of trees. Collect a leaf from each tree and do rubbings of them and from the bark by placing a sheet of paper over them and rubbing it with the side of a crayon. Gather as much information as you can on each tree. Measure the tree around its widest point. If you can, take a photograph of the tree or draw a picture of the tree, showing the type of branches, whether the tree is short, tall, narrow, or full. Note the type of bark—thick, rough, smooth, papery, scaly, or flaky and its color—reddish, green, brown, black, grey, or tan. Note whether it has needles, buds, or flowers and whether it is bare or full of leaves; if full, describe the color of the leaves.

Conclusion/What is going on? Complete a table showing the time of year, the name of the tree, a description of the tree's bark, leaves, and general appearance, and include leaf rubbings, photographs, and drawings. Try to find as many types of trees as you can.

Report and Present: Write out the steps and what you saw. Display your chart, rubbings, photographs, and drawings.

Tree Growth

Hypothesis or Statement of Purpose: To understand how trees grow and how environment affects their growth.

What you need:

   Twigs or small branches from different types of trees

   Tape measurer

Test, watch, and record: Find twigs that have fallen from different trees in different locations. Note the number of sections on the twig to see how many growth seasons are visible. Sketch or photograph the tree and gather info about it and the environment. Do other trees compete with it for water or sunlight? Is there evidence of bad drainage or extra water from sprinklers? Measure each segment on the twig and record the data. Find which year had least growth; most growth. Find an average growth for that year. Compare different twigs. Many trees grow 1 inch around each year, so estimate the age of a tree by measuring around the tree at about 5 feet up from the ground. Divide that figure by 1 inch to estimate the tree's age.

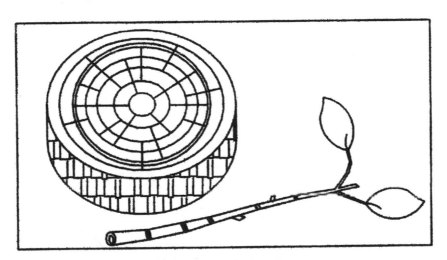

Conclusion/What is going on? Trees grow taller and fuller from the tips of branches and deeper from the roots. Another layer of cells increases the width of the trunk to support the tree and provide a way for water to reach branches. While alive, growth can be seen by measuring the diameter of the trunk and seeing growth on branches. Each spring, trees bud at the end of twigs to begin the year's growth. Then the remaining part of the bud creates a scar or ring. When cut, a tree trunk's growth rings can be seen. Each year a tree produces new xylem (vertical tube cells) near the outer layer of the trunk. In the wet spring, the tree produces large xylem cells; smaller cells in the dry summer, and few cells in winter when water is scarce. The pattern of fast and slow growth causes dark and light rings. Each ring represents a growing season.

Report and Present: Write out the steps and what you saw. Explain the results using "What is going on?" above to help you. Display twigs and drawings or photos.

From Carol Peterson, *Jump into Science: Themed Science Fairs*. Westport, CT: Teacher Ideas Press. © 2007 by Carol Peterson.

Tracking Station

Hypothesis or Statement of Purpose: To understand what types of animals or insects live in your ecosystem.

What you need:

Wooden board about 3 feet by 3 feet   Spoon
Soft dirt   Peanut butter
Small block of wood about 4 inches by 4
     inches

Test, watch, and record: Before dark, locate a place in your garden near trees, bushes, or grass. Place a board on the ground and cover it with about ½ inch of dirt. Make sure the edges are covered. Place a wood block in the middle, and spoon a mound of peanut butter on top. The next morning, look for footprints or other evidence of creatures that might have visited your station. Sketch or photograph the footprints. If no creatures visited your station, take it to a park or field and try it again. Try to determine which creature or creatures made the tracks. Explain your reasoning.

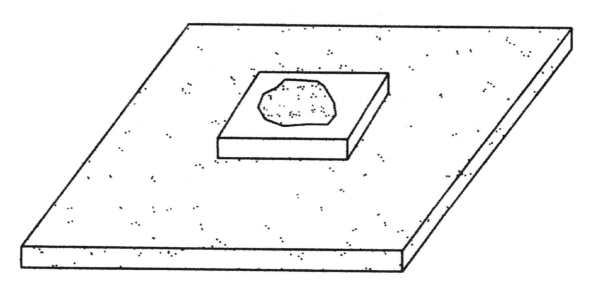

Conclusion/What is going on? Report and Present: Write out the steps and what you saw. Explain the results using "What is going on?" above to help you. Display your sketches or photographs.

 From Carol Peterson, *Jump into Science: Themed Science Fairs*. Westport, CT: Teacher Ideas Press.

Water Cycle

Hypothesis or Statement of Purpose: To understand how temperature affects the cycle of water.

What you need:

Three jars or bowls the same size   Measuring cup
6 cups of water   Flexible lamp
Ten ice cubes   Labels
Ice chest   Marking pen
Thermometer

Test, watch, and record: Label one container "Cool," a second "Warm," and a third "Control." Measure 2 cups of water into the "Warm" and "Control" jars. Place 10 ice cubes in the "Cool" jar and add enough water to bring the level up to the other two jars. Mark the water level in each jar. Record the temperature of the room. Then place the thermometer in each jar for 5 minutes and record the temperature of the water in the jars. Place the "Cool" jar inside the ice chest. Shine the light onto the "Warm" jar for 1 hour and then record the temperature of the "Warm" water. Turn off the lamp. Let all three containers sit for 24 hours. Observe and mark the new water level in each jar. Compare the ending and beginning levels.

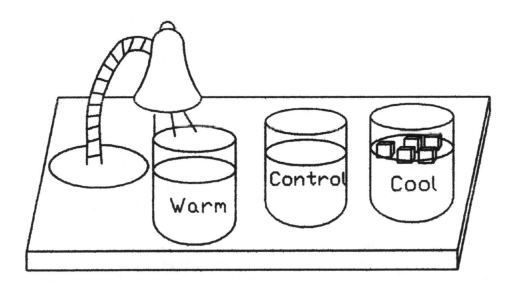

Conclusion/What is going on? The temperature of the water, the temperature of the air around the water, and the amount of water in the container affect evaporation. We kept the amount of water in all three containers equal. You found that the jar in which the water and air around it were warm showed the most evaporation.

Report and Present: Write out the steps and what you saw. Explain the results using "What is going on?" above to help you. Display your jars and data table.

Water Percolation

Hypothesis or Statement of Purpose: To understand how water moves underground.

What you need:

One jar, quart-sized or larger   Spoon
2 cups sand   ½ cup water
2 cups gravel

Test, watch, and record: Outside, mix sand and gravel in the jar with the spoon. Slowly pour the water over the sand and gravel. Observe the water as it moves through the jar. Let the jar stand in a warm place for 4 days and observe the sand and gravel, including its wetness.

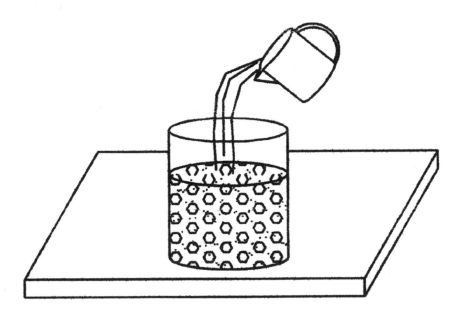

Conclusion/What is going on? As the water moves through the sand and gravel, it fills air pockets. As the water flows to the bottom of the jar, the water in those spaces filters to the sand and gravel at the bottom of the jar. Over time, the upper layer becomes dry, while the sand and gravel at the bottom remains wet. Rainwater filters through the rocks and soil in a similar way; called "percolation." Gravity pulls the water down until it reaches and spreads out over a layer where it can no longer pass through. This "impermeable" layer is represented by the jar.

Report and Present: Write out the steps and what you saw. Explain the results using "What is going on?" above to help you. Display your jar. Or spread the sand and gravel out to dry and repeat the experiment to show the water percolation.

Acid/Neutral Plant Growth

Hypothesis or Statement of Purpose: To understand the effect of acids and bases on plants.

What you need:

Vinegar   Labels or tape
Water   Marking pen
Two jars of equal size   Measuring cup
Two cuttings about the same size from   Measuring spoon
    the same plant

Test, watch, and record: Measure an equal amount of water into each jar. Using the marking pen, label one jar "acid" and 1 jar "control." To the acid jar, stir in 1 tablespoon of vinegar. Place one plant cutting into each jar. Let the cuttings sit in a sunny place for 2 weeks.

Conclusion/What is going on? Rainwater is slightly acidic. When fuel is burned in our cars and factories, some of the waste combines with water in the air to form acids that fall to the ground in rain or dry specks. This experiment shows how higher acid in the water can affect plants.

Report and Present: Write out the steps and what you saw. Explain the results using "What is going on?" above to help you. Display your plant cuttings.

From Carol Peterson, *Jump into Science: Themed Science Fairs*. Westport, CT: Teacher Ideas Press.
© 2007 by Carol Peterson.

Weathervane

Hypothesis or Statement of Purpose: To understand how to determine wind direction.

What you need:

Sheet of construction paper	Funnel
Wire cutters	Scissors
Plastic drinking straw	Glue
Heavy nail	Pencil
Stiff wire (about 14-16 inches)	Small paperclip
Hammer	Duct or masking tape
20-ounce soda bottle with plastic screw top	Strips of paper approximately 3 to 4 inches wide
Wood block	Black markers
Sand	Magnetic compass

Test, watch, and record: Fold the paper in half to make a rectangle 8½ by 5½ inches. Sketch a shape on one side and cut through both papers to make two matching shapes. Tape the straw to the inside of the center of one shape so it extends below the shape by 1 or 2 inches. Cut off any straw above the top. Tape the top end of the drinking straw closed. Tape a paperclip to the back end of the shape and glue the second shape to the first, matching edges. Let dry.

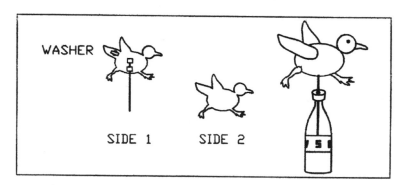

WASHER   SIDE 1   SIDE 2

With a funnel, fill the bottle with sand. Cut and tape a band of paper around the bottle and write an "N" on the paper on one side of the bottle, then an "E," an "S," and a "W" around the bottle to form a compass. Set the bottle cap on the wood and hammer a nail through the center of the cap to make a hole. Remove the nail and screw the cap back on the bottle. Cut a length of wire as tall as the bottle plus the height of the shape. Insert the wire through the bottle cap and into the sand. Slide the straw and shape over the wire. Make sure the shape spins freely. Outside, point the N on your bottle north. If you don't have a compass, think about the direction the sun rises (east) and sets (west). When you are facing north, east will be on your right and west will be on your left.

Conclusion/What is going on? One half of the weathervane is heavier than the other. As wind blows against the weathervane, the heavy part resists the wind and turns away. The light end turns into the wind, pointing to the direction the wind comes from.

Report and Present: Write out the steps and what you saw. Explain the results using "What is going on?" above to help you. Think about how knowing wind direction helps people know what kind of weather is coming.

Weather Station

Hypothesis or Statement of Purpose: To understand patterns of weather.

What you need:

Thermometer

Windsock or light fabric hung freely

Compass

Clock

Cup and ruler (to measure precipitation)

Daily newspaper or access to weather report on TV, radio, or Internet

Test, watch, and record: Create a data chart. Include date, time, temperature, sky (clear, overcast), cloud cover (type or description), wind (direction, calm, breeze, strong), precipitation (type and amount). Think of other information you might gather. Collect data several times a day at the same time, for 1 to 2 weeks. Compare your data with official weather information.

Conclusion/What is going on? There are many things that create our weather. By collecting data several times a day over a period of time, you will begin to see patterns—for example, how certain temperatures and cloud patterns occur when the weather is clear or when it is rainy. This project will help you be more aware of weather factors and what they mean.

Report and Present: Write out the steps and what you saw. Explain the results using "What is going on?" above to help you. Display your data chart. Cover one column and ask students what they would expect that data to show based on other information.

From Carol Peterson, *Jump into Science: Themed Science Fairs*. Westport, CT: Teacher Ideas Press. © 2007 by Carol Peterson.

Erosion

Hypothesis or Statement of Purpose: To understand soil erosion through water.

What you need:

A large aluminum foil cooking sheet
Sharp nail
Sand or sandy garden soil

Lids from small jars and bottles of various sizes
Spray bottle of water

Test, watch, and record: Outside, poke several dozen holes in the bottom of the foil sheet with the nail. Fill the sheet with sand. Place the lids on top of the sand and press down gently. Spray the sand with the water bottle until the sand is completely wet. Allow the water to drain and continue to sprinkle, making sure not to flood the tray. Allow the water to dry overnight and then spray again. Continue to spray and let dry for 1 week. At the end of the week, remove the lids from the soil. Record your observations.

Conclusion/What is going on? The sand under the lids formed pedestals as the sand around it washed away. Wind, ice, water, and soil can all cause erosion. This type of water erosion is called "sheet erosion." Water from higher elevations washes away fine soil and leaves denser materials underneath. This type of landscape can be found in the Arizona desert.

Report and Present: Write out the steps and what you saw. Explain the results using "What is going on?" above to help you. If you wish to display your "eroded landscape," carefully spray it with clear varnish to help protect it. If you cannot spray it, make diagrams showing the steps in the experiment and the stages of erosion. Display photographs of landscapes in nature that are examples of this and other types of erosion.

PRESERVING OUR RESOURCES

 Composting

Hypothesis or Statement of Purpose: To understand how materials decompose.

What you need:

Two 1-gallon-sized plastic bags	Marking pen
Pencil	Masking tape or labels
Two paper or Styrofoam food containers	3–5 cups soil
Two glass bottles	Plastic gloves
Two pieces leftover food	Newspaper
Two small leaves	Water
Two metal cans	

Test, watch, and record: Allow at least one month for this experiment. Punch 20 small holes into both bags with the pencil. Make a list of items going into the bags. In one bag, place one of each item. Sprinkle lightly with water but do not add soil. Tie the bag closed and label it "control." Fill the second bag with the other items. Add soil and sprinkle with water. Tie the bag closed and label it "test." Place both bags outside in the shade. Open each bag every 2 weeks, sprinkle with water, and retie. Record your observations. After 1 month, open both bags. Wearing rubber gloves, pour the contents onto a newspaper next to each other. Compare the changes in each item inside the control and test bags.

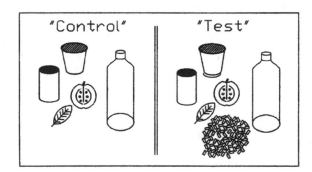

Conclusion/What is going on? Composting is a process in which organic (living) matter is broken down to become rich soil called "humus." Good soil is made by the action of microorganisms, bacteria, and fungi that break down waste. Organic waste includes leaves, vegetables, paper bags, grass clippings, and coffee grounds. The carbon in those items provides food for microorganisms. The carbon is burned off, causing the pile to heat up, killing harmful organisms. Macro-organisms (earthworms, insects, mites, grubs—organisms that are large enough to see with the eye) chew the organic matter into smaller pieces. Their digestion and excretion release chemicals into the compost, which becomes humus. A sanitary landfill is a place where materials are covered with soil to encourage decomposition.

Report and Present: Write out the steps and what you saw. Explain the results using "What is going on?" above to help you. Take photographs or make drawings of the stages of the composting to display along with your notes and list of items in each bag. Consider how an understanding of composting could be used in gardening.

From Carol Peterson, *Jump into Science: Themed Science Fairs*. Westport, CT: Teacher Ideas Press. © 2007 by Carol Peterson.

Make Your Own Paper

Hypothesis or Statement of Purpose: To understand how paper can be recycled into new paper.

What you need:

Old newspapers	Eggbeater
Large square or rectangular pan or plastic tub	Large spoon
	Cup
Screen about 4 inches square	Water

Test, watch, and record: Rip newspaper into tiny pieces and place in bowl. Cover with water and soak for 2 hours. Beat with eggbeater for 10 minutes until newspaper becomes mush. Place screen in bottom of pan. Pour mush over screen. Lift screen out of the pan to gather a sheet of mush as you lift. Fill any holes with more mush. Hold the screen over the pan to drain extra water. Then set the screen of mush onto a newspaper. Cover with more newspaper. Press to remove some of the water. Uncover the screen and dry overnight. Peel the paper from the screen.

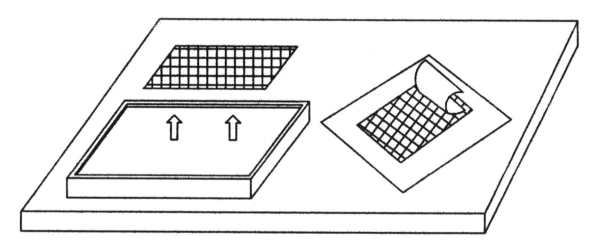

Conclusion/What is going on? Paper consists of wood pulp, called "lignum." When the paper is soaked, it breaks apart into fiber that can be mixed. But when the water is dried, the fibers lock together again. Many papermakers use some recycled paper to make new paper.

Report and Present: Write out the steps and what you saw. Explain the results using "What is going on?" above to help you. Display some of the original paper and the paper you made.

From Carol Peterson, *Jump into Science: Themed Science Fairs*. Westport, CT: Teacher Ideas Press.
© 2007 by Carol Peterson.

Recycling (Glass, Paper, Metal, Organics)

Hypothesis or Statement of Purpose: To understand the importance of recycling.

What you need:

    1 week's worth of family garbage

Test, watch, and record: Take charge of collecting the garbage for your family for 1 week. Record the number of cans, glass bottles, and plastic bottles thrown away. Also record the number of bags of garbage in 1 week. Estimate the amount of garbage that is paper, plastic, and organic material. Multiply the number of bags of garbage by 52 for the number of bags of garbage your family makes in 1 year. Divide the number of bags each week by the number of people in your family to find out how much garbage each person makes. Find out what type of recycling program is available in your community. Determine how your family can participate in the program, if you do not already, and how much organic material you can use for composting in your garden.

Conclusion/What is going on? We are not always aware of how much garbage we create. The use of our land to store garbage may not be its best use. Becoming aware of the amount of garbage is the first step to reducing it. Participating in recycling so that our garbage has less long-term effects is a second step.

Report and Present: Write out the steps you used in this experiment and what you saw. Explain the results using "What is going on?" above to help you. Present ways you can encourage your family and community to recycle.

From Carol Peterson, *Jump into Science: Themed Science Fairs*. Westport, CT: Teacher Ideas Press. © 2007 by Carol Peterson.

Magnetic Spring

Hypothesis or Statement of Purpose: To understand how magnetism has a functional use.

What you need:

> Five bar magnets
>
> Six pencils
>
> Styrofoam block about 6 inches long, 3 inches wide, and 2 inches high

Test, watch, and record: Lay one bar magnet in the center of the Styrofoam horizontally. Poke the pencils around the edge to form a cage for the magnets—two on each long side and one on each end of the block. Remove the magnet and then arrange all of the magnets in a stack inside the pencil cage so each magnet pushes away from the magnet above it. Press down on the top magnet and observe how the magnets react. Record your observations.

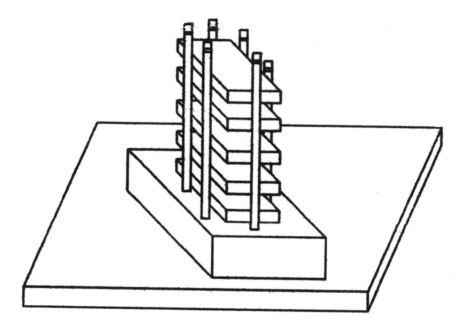

Conclusion/What is going on? Pressing down on the stack feels like a spring. Magnets attract each other when the opposite poles are brought together. Magnets repel against each other when south poles or north poles are together. The north and south poles of these magnets are lined up so that they repel each other.

Report and Present: Write out the steps and what you saw. Explain the results using "What is going on?" above to help you. This technology is used in trains that float above the ground using magnetism. How would using this technology help with issues of alternative energy?

From Carol Peterson, *Jump into Science: Themed Science Fairs*. Westport, CT: Teacher Ideas Press.
© 2007 by Carol Peterson.

Solar Collector

Hypothesis or Statement of Purpose: To understand how the sun can be used for energy.

What you need:

Three glass jars the same size   Scissors
Masking tape   Nail
Three outdoor thermometers   Pencil
Aluminum foil   Watch
Black construction paper   Water
Poster board or thin cardboard

Test, watch, and record: Trace around each jar mouth onto cardboard and cut out. Poke a hole in the center of each circle with a nail. Fill the jars with water. Slide a thermometer through each hole. Tape a cardboard circle on top of each jar. Adjust thermometers so they can be read. Tape thermometers in place, so they do not touch the side or bottom of the jar. Wrap one jar in black paper and tape paper in place. Wrap one jar in foil. Leave the third jar unwrapped. Record the temperature of each jar. Place jars in the sun. Record the temperature of each jar after 1 minute, 10 minutes, 20 minutes, and 30 minutes. Create a data table showing: time, temperature in plain jar, temperature in foil jar, and temperature in black jar

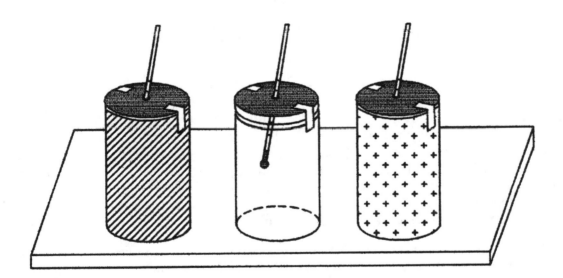

Conclusion/What is going on? The beginning temperatures of all bottles should be the same. Dark colors absorb and hold heat. Light or shiny material reflects light and heat away from it. The jar covered in black should record the highest temperature. The foil-covered jar should record the lowest temperature. The uncovered jar should show a temperature between the two.

Report and Present: Write out the steps and what you saw. Explain the results using "What is going on?" above to help you. Display your jars and data table.

Turbine Engines

Hypothesis or Statement of Purpose: To understand how water can create electricity.

What you need:

      Pinwheel

      Access to running water

Test, watch, and record: Hold the pinwheel under a stream of water. As the water hits the pinwheel, the force of the water turns the pinwheel.

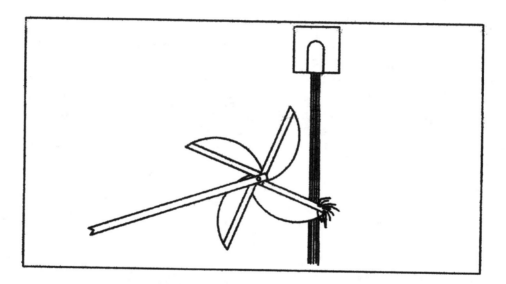

Conclusion/What is going on? Moving water has "inertia" which means it tends to keep going and applies force against anything that is in its way. The faster water moves, the more force it has. Large bodies of water can use engines like a pinwheel. To create electricity, a dam at one end of a body of water blocks the water's flow. The water at the surface pushes on the water at the bottom, building more pressure as water keeps coming toward the dam without flowing out. At the bottom of the dam, pipes allow the built-up water to rush through them to turn giant wheels called "turbines." These turbines then move generators, which create electrical current.

Report and Present: Write out the steps and what you saw. Explain the results using "What is going on?" above to help you. Display your pinwheel and photographs or drawings of a turbine engine. Relate this to windmills that use wind to create electricity.

 From Carol Peterson, *Jump into Science: Themed Science Fairs*. Westport, CT: Teacher Ideas Press. © 2007 by Carol Peterson.

Hydroponics

Hypothesis or Statement of Purpose: To understand how plants can grow in water.

What you need:

Potato	Two flat sponges
Carrot with leaves	Toothpicks
Grass seed	Aluminum foil
Drinking glass or jar	Knife
Saucer	

Test, watch, and record: Carefully cut potato in half. Poke four toothpicks into the potato halfway up from the cut end. Fill a glass or jar with water. Set the potato into it so the cut side is under the water and toothpicks support the top. Cut the top of a carrot off near the leaves. Fill a saucer with water. Place the carrot top in the saucer with the leaves up. Wet the sponges with water. Place one sponge on the foil and sprinkle with grass seed. Place the second sponge on top of the first. Place all three in a sunny spot and let them sit for 3 days. Record your observations.

Conclusion/What is going on? We assume plants need fertile soil to grow. Within a few days you should see that the potato, the carrot, and the seed in between the sponges have sprouted. Later these can be planted in soil and fertilized. Think how using hydroponics might relate to farming in the future on Earth or in space.

Report and Present: Write out the steps and what you saw. Explain the results using "What is going on?" above to help you. Display your plantings.

From Carol Peterson, *Jump into Science: Themed Science Fairs*. Westport, CT: Teacher Ideas Press. © 2007 by Carol Peterson.

OUR WORLD AT RISK

  ## Cleaning Water

Hypothesis or Statement of Purpose: To understand how polluted water might be made safe.

What you need:

1 gallon swamp water (or add 2 cups dirt to a gallon of tap water)
Bucket
Three large clear plastic soda bottles
1 cup fine sand

1 cup coarse sand
2 cups washed gravel or pebbles
Coffee filter
Rubber band
Tap water

Test, watch, and record: Do this outside. Have an adult remove the bottom third of one of the soda bottles with a saw or sharp knife. Nearly fill an uncut bottle with swamp water, using the cut bottle top as a funnel. Observe how the water looks and smells. Rinse out the swamp-water bucket with tap water. Place the cap on the bottle filled with swamp water and shake for 30 seconds. Pour the water back and forth between the two uncut bottles 12 times. Record any changes in the water.

Wrap the coffee filter around the top of the cut bottle and secure with a rubber band. Turn the bottle top upside down and layer fine sand, then coarse sand, then pebbles inside. Hold the bottle top over the bucket. Pour half of the shaken water over the pebbles in the bottle top. Record your observations about the look and smell of the filtered water compared with the untreated water.

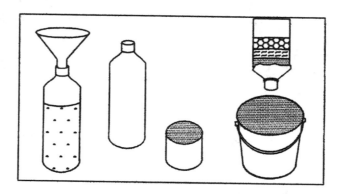

Conclusion/What is going on? Shaking releases gases from the water and adds oxygen. This is called "aerating" the water. The sand, rocks, and filter remove particles to clean the water. DO NOT DRINK the treated water. Although it looks clean, it may still contain harmful organisms. Treatment companies add chemicals to kill these organisms before the water is safe to drink.

Report and Present: Write out the steps and what you saw. Explain the results using "What is going on?" above to help you. Keep a small amount of swamp water and treated water in bottles to show other students the difference.

Dissolved Oxygen

Hypothesis or Statement of Purpose: To understand how levels of oxygen in water affect life.

What you need:

Three large clear soda bottles

A rotting banana

1–2 gallons of untreated water from a lake, stream, river, or pond

Marking pen

Large spoon

Plastic knife

Funnel

Test, watch, and record: With a marker, label the bottles "Low," "High," and "Control." Stir water quickly for 5 minutes. With a funnel, fill the bottles with water. Record your observations about the water. Cut the banana into three equal pieces. Slice further if needed so pieces fit through the bottle openings. Place one-third of the banana into the "High" bottle. Place two-thirds of the banana into the "Low" bottle. Do not place anything in the "Control" bottle. Set the bottles in a warm place for 5 days. Record the condition of the water each day.

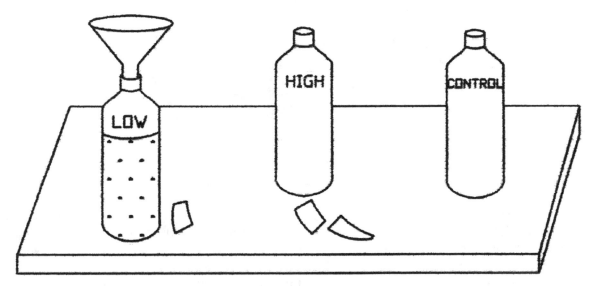

Conclusion/What is going on? Many things affect the level of oxygen in water—the amount of plant photosynthesis, the number of fish breathing oxygen from the water, the temperature, the amount of salt, and the amount of decaying matter in the water. The more decaying matter, the lower the level of dissolved oxygen. A low level of oxygen kills life that lives in water. If there is too little oxygen for fish and other life, the body of water can become a dead zone.

Report and Present: Write out the steps and what you saw. Explain the results using "What is going on?" above to help you. Display your three bottles.

From Carol Peterson, *Jump into Science: Themed Science Fairs*. Westport, CT: Teacher Ideas Press. © 2007 by Carol Peterson.

Greenhouse Effect

Hypothesis or Statement of Purpose: To understand how the greenhouse effect may influence global warming.

What you need:

Two thermometers	Plastic wrap
Thick cardboard box	Tape

Test, watch, and record: Place one thermometer inside the box so it can be seen. Cover with the plastic and tape plastic securely. Place the box in the sun. Set the second thermometer next to the box. Record the temperature inside and outside the box at same time morning, afternoon, and evening for 7 days, if possible. Observe and record the temperature and the weather conditions.

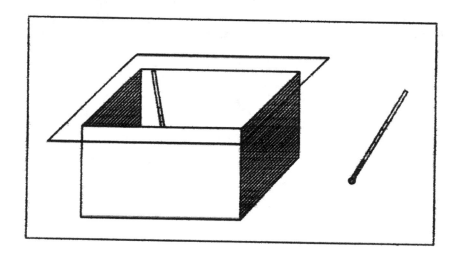

Conclusion/What is going on? Our atmosphere keeps heat within it like glass does in a greenhouse. Warm sunlight passes through our atmosphere and hits the land and water, which hold the heat. Some of the heat returns up to the atmosphere by infrared radiation. In the atmosphere, it is absorbed by gases there, such as carbon dioxide. Water in the air also traps heat in the atmosphere and contributes to the greenhouse effect. The result is that more heat is trapped, and the surface of the Earth stays warm. There is a theory that warmer temperature could cause climate changes. Because fossil fuels in our gasoline contain carbon dioxide, this theory says that more carbon dioxide will speed up the warming of Earth.

Report and Present: Write out the steps and what you saw. Explain the results using "What is going on?" above to help you. Display your box and data table.

Groundwater Pollution

Hypothesis or Statement of Purpose: To understand how groundwater can become polluted.

What you need:

Large, clear plastic container at least 6
   inches deep
1 pound modeling clay
1 pound sand
2 pounds rinsed gravel
Plastic straw

Spray bottle
Green felt 3 inches by 5 inches
¼ cup red powdered drink mix, such as Kool-Aid
Red food coloring
Clean water
Tape

Test, watch, and record: Tape the straw vertically to the inside of a plastic container slightly up from the bottom. The straw represents a well to groundwater. Pour 2 inches of sand on the bottom of the container. Wet the sand with about ½ cup water. This represents an aquifer. Flatten clay into a thin sheet. Cover half of the sand with clay, pressing it against three sides of the container. The clay represents a solid layer of rock. Pour a small amount of water onto the clay. Most of the water should puddle on top of the clay. Sprinkle gravel over everything, forming a hill on one side of the container. Pour water into the container until it is even with bottom of the hill, to form a lake. Drop red food coloring through the straw to show how pollution travels through a well into an aquifer. Sprinkle the hill with powdered soft drink, to represent chemical fertilizers. Spray the hill to show how rain can cause fertilizers to enter the surface water.

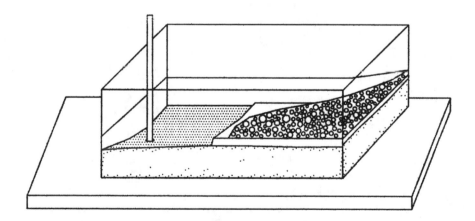

Conclusion/What is going on? Groundwater can be an underground lake or river. As rain falls on the surface, some of it filters through the surface and into the ground. Aquifers collect this groundwater in permeable rock, which is made of loose material. Eventually the water will travel until it reaches a solid layer of rock. The water table is the upper surface of the groundwater. Groundwater and surface water can become polluted from leaking underground tanks, from septic systems, from fertilizer runoff, and chemicals from factories

Report and Present: Write out the steps and what you saw. Explain the results using "What is going on?" above to help you. Display your model.

From Carol Peterson, *Jump into Science: Themed Science Fairs*. Westport, CT: Teacher Ideas Press.
© 2007 by Carol Peterson.

Soil Pollution

Hypothesis or Statement of Purpose: To understand the effect of household cleaners on plant growth.

What you need:

- Two potted plants of the same size and variety
- Two dishes underneath the pots
- Measuring cup
- Dishwashing liquid
- Spoon
- Two labels
- Pen

Test, watch, and record: Place two potted plants in a window where they can receive adequate sunlight. Make sure the two plants are the same variety and the same size and health. Label one pot "Control." Label the second plant "Polluted." Measure one cup of tap water and pour over the soil of the "Control" plant. Place several drops of liquid dishwashing detergent into the measuring cup and add one cup of tap water. Stir to dissolve the detergent. Then pour the water over the soil of the "Polluted" plant. Rinse the measuring cup thoroughly and drain off whatever water has gathered in the dishes under the pots. Check the soil every few days. If it appears dry, add more water—plain water to the "Control" plant and detergent water to the "Polluted" plant. Do not overwater either plant and make sure to drain extra water from the dishes. Record your observations about each plant for 2 weeks.

Conclusion/What is going on? The detergent in the water should make the "Polluted" plant unhealthy. Detergent and other household cleaners contain chemicals that are harmful to plants. They can enter the ecosystem through storm drains and affect both the water and the soil. Think about how this could affect our food supply.

Report and Present: Write out the steps and what you saw. Explain the results using "What is going on?" above to help you. Display both plants.

Pollution in Your Air

Hypothesis or Statement of Purpose: To understand that our air contains tiny particles.

What you need:

Large can or deep bowl

Plain white paper towel

Magnifying glass

Test, watch, and record: Place the paper towel inside the can or bowl and set it outside in a location that is protected from rain. Tape the paper towel to the can if needed to keep it from blowing away. Let the can sit for 1 week. Remove the paper towel and look at it through the magnifying glass. Record your observations and make drawings of what you see.

Conclusion/What is going on? The air carries small particles in it. Some of these are pollen, soil, or other particles from nature. The air also carries particles of pollution from cars and factories. The particles in the air can sometimes form a haze, which we see and which can cause irritation to eyes, lungs, and airways.

Report and Present: Write out the steps and what you saw. Explain the results using "What is going on?" above to help you. Place your paper towel in a zippered plastic bag and display it and your drawings of the particles. Let other students use the magnifying glass to observe particles.

From Carol Peterson, *Jump into Science: Themed Science Fairs*. Westport, CT: Teacher Ideas Press. © 2007 by Carol Peterson.

Levels of Erosion

Hypothesis or Statement of Purpose: To understand soil erosion through water.

What you need:

Three square or rectangular aluminum foil cooking pans of equal size

Sand or sandy garden soil

2 cups of mulch, straw, or wood bark

Sod to fit the pan or 6 to 8 small plants

Block of wood 2 inches by 4 inches, about 6 inches long

Quart measuring cup

Three 1-quart containers

Scissors

Felt-tip pen

Test, watch, and record: Do this outside. Label the pans and the three containers "1," "2," and "3." With scissors, cut a V-shaped notch in the center of one side of each pan, as shown. Rebend the foil if needed to return the pan to its shape. Fill each pan with equal amounts of soil, using the measuring cup. Record the amount of soil used. Level and press the soil into place in each pan with your hand. Sprinkle the mulch, straw, or bark on the top of the soil in pan "1." Cut the sod to fit pan "2" or plant the small plants deep in the soil, pressing in place. Leave the soil in pan "3" undisturbed. Now place pan "1" on the wood block so that the notched end is lower than the back. Place the container underneath the notch. Measure and pour 3 cups of water over the soil at the back of the pan, allowing the water to flow through the soil, out the notch, and into the container. Let the water drain completely. Pour the water from the container into the measuring cup. Record that measurement. Then pour the water from the measuring cup back into the container. Repeat this process for the second and third pans. Compare the water in each container and the amount of soil it contains. Record your observations.

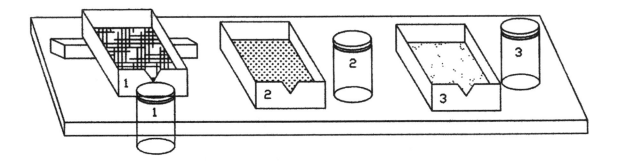

Conclusion/What is going on? The pan with the sod or plants should have lost the least water and soil. The pan with only the soil should have lost the most water and soil. The sod and plants contained roots, which held the soil and stopped it from being carried away with the water. The mulch on top of the soil helped slow down the erosion, but not as well as the plant roots. Think about how humans changing natural landscapes may affect erosion levels.

Report and Present: Write out the steps and what you saw. Explain the results using "What is going on?" above to help you. Display your boxes and the jars of soil and water.

 From Carol Peterson, *Jump into Science: Themed Science Fairs*. Westport, CT: Teacher Ideas Press. © 2007 by Carol Peterson.

LIFE SCIENCE UNIT

Organisms, Insects, and Animals

Plants

Humans

ORGANISMS, INSECTS, AND ANIMALS

Growing Bacteria

Hypothesis or Statement of Purpose: To understand bacterial fermentation.

What you need:

5 cups milk	Whisk or eggbeater
¼ cup plain yogurt *with active cultures*	Oven-safe dish
Measuring cup	Oven, crock-pot or electric fry pan

Test, watch, and record: Wash your hands with soap and water. Heat the milk in a microwave or on the stove until it is warm but not hot. Add the active yogurt and beat thoroughly with a whisk or eggbeater. The mixture must then "incubate." This means it must be kept warm but not hot for a certain amount of time so the good bacteria can grow. To incubate your yogurt you can place it in an ovenproof pan in a 100-degree oven for 6 to 8 hours. Or you can place it in a crock-pot set on low, turning the crock-pot on for 10 minutes and off for 30 minutes for 6 to 8 hours. Or you can place the dish in an electric frying pan filled with water and set at 100 degrees for 6 to 8 hours. Then store your yogurt in the refrigerator. It should be eaten within a few days.

Conclusion/What is going on? Fermentation is a chemical change of sugar into either alcohol (such as in wine or beer) or acid (such as in cheese and yogurt). To make yogurt, a special type of bacteria eats the milk sugars and releases lactic acid. This acid prevents other, harmful bacteria from growing in the milk. Using low heat while making yogurt keeps good bacteria ("active cultures") alive. It can be used to grow bacteria in future batches of yogurt.

Report and Present: Write out the steps and what you saw. Explain the results using "What is going on?" above to help you. If you can keep the yogurt cold, prepare it a day or two before the presentation and serve samples.

From Carol Peterson, *Jump into Science: Themed Science Fairs*. Westport, CT: Teacher Ideas Press.
© 2007 by Carol Peterson.

Growing Organisms

Hypothesis or Statement of Purpose: To understand how organisms grow.

What you need:

Two small jars with covers	Measuring spoons
Two packages yeast	Spoon
One large soda bottle	Water
4 tablespoons sugar	Balloon

Test, watch, and record: Half fill two jars with warm water. Stir 1 teaspoon of sugar into one jar. Sprinkle ¼ teaspoon yeast into each jar. Cover jars and let them sit for 30 minutes. Record your observations. Fill the bottle half way with warm water. Add 3 tablespoons sugar and a package of yeast. Cover and shake. Remove cap and slip the end of the balloon over the bottle opening. Let the bottle sit for 20 minutes and observe. Let bottle sit another half hour. Record your observations, including the smell.

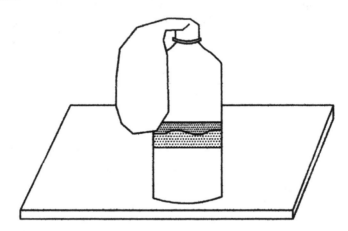

Conclusion/What is going on? The yeast sank in the jar with no sugar. In the jar with sugar, it rose to the top and foamed. The bubbles are carbon dioxide. The balloon expands to show this gas. When making bread, yeast eats the sugar in the dough. The resulting carbon dioxide bubbles cause the dough to rise. Baking locks the air pockets in the bread.

Organisms reproduce to survive. Some organisms split in two, a process called "fission." Other organisms, such as mushrooms, produce single-celled "spores" that grow new organisms. Yeast reproduces by "budding." A portion of a cell grows out and forms a bud. The wall between the bud and the cell then closes until the bud separates into a new cell. If you have a microscope, observe some of the yeast mixture.

Report and Present: Write out the steps and what you saw. Explain the results using "What is going on?" above to help you. Display drawings of the stages of your experiment. Display a slice of bread to show the air pockets.

Molds

Hypothesis or Statement of Purpose: To understand how molds grow.

What you need:

    Slice of bread   Slice of cheese (not processed)

    Slice of ripe fruit   Three jars with lids

Test, watch, and record: Place a slice of bread in one jar, a slice of fruit in the second jar, and a slice of cheese in the third jar. Secure the tops. Place jars in a cool dark place for one week. Compare the contents and record your observations. DO NOT OPEN JARS. After your presentation, dispose of jars to avoid contact with the molds.

Conclusion/What is going on? Some molds are helpful, such as in certain cheeses, as well as penicillin, which is a mold used to make a helpful medicine. Other molds from spoiled food or growing in moist areas in homes can be harmful to people if eaten, inhaled, or touched.

Report and Present: Write out the steps and what you saw. Explain the results using "What is going on?" above to help you. Display your jars of moldy food.

How Microbes Can Spread Infection

Hypothesis or Statement of Purpose: To understand how infections can spread.

What you need:

Bruised apple beginning to decay	Water
Seven fresh apples	Soap
Six zippered plastic bags	Alcohol
Fork	Paper towels
Marking pen	

Test, watch, and record: Five days ahead of time, hit an apple several times against the table to bruise it. Set it in a warm, dark place. On day five, label plastic bags "1" through "5." Label the sixth bag "Control." Place one apple in the control bag. Set a second apple to one side as a second control. Rub the decaying apple over the 5 other apples. Throw away the decaying apple. Wash hands with soap and water.

Place one of the rubbed apples in bag 1. Drop a second rubbed apple against the table several times to bruise it and place it in bag 2. Poke a third apple several times with a fork and place it in bag 3. Wash the fourth apple with soap and water. Dry it with a paper towel and place it in bag 4. Wash the fifth apple with alcohol. Dry it with a paper towel and place it in bag 5. Wash your hands again with soap and water. Record bruises, breaks in the skin, and anything else you observe about each apple. Place all apples in a warm, dark place for 1 week. Then examine the apples. Compare the two control apples and compare the apples in bags 1–5 with the two controls. Record your observations.

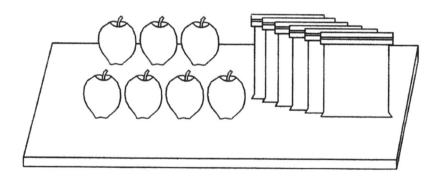

Conclusion/What is going on? The control apples let you compare infected and uninfected apples and see whether the plastic affects rotting. The two controls should have no change. Apple #1 should show some rotting. Apple #2 should show severe rotting. Apple #3 should show rotting where the skin was punctured. Apple #4 should show discoloration. Apple #5 should show no change. The apple skin protects it from rotting by making it hard for bacteria to attack the inside. Washing removes bacteria from the surface so that decay does not begin. Alcohol kills bacteria, which is why a doctor wipes your skin with alcohol before giving you a shot. This experiment shows the effects of bacteria and how to help or slow their spread.

Report and Present: Write out the steps and what you saw. Explain the results using "What is going on?" above to help you. Display your 7 apples.

Membranes

Hypothesis or Statement of Purpose: To understand the qualities of membranes.

What you need:

One or two raw eggs in their shell	Corn syrup
One or two jars with lids	Paper towels
White vinegar	

Test, watch, and record: Pour 1 cup of vinegar into a jar. Tilt the jar and slide the egg to the bottom of the jar so that you don't crack the shell. Raise the jar upright. Add enough vinegar to cover the egg. Close the lid. Observe the egg for 15 minutes and record your observations. Leave the egg in the vinegar for 5 days. Each day record changes in the egg or what is happening in the jar. Then unscrew the lid. Hold the lid with one hand and drain the vinegar into the sink so the egg stays in the jar. Gently slide the egg onto a paper towel. Poke the egg with your finger and observe how it has changed. Record your observations. Return the egg to the jar and cover with more vinegar for your presentation, securing the lid so the egg will not smell.

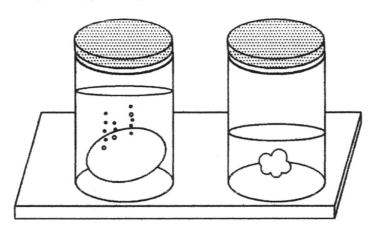

If desired, experiment with two eggs in vinegar and place one of the two dissolved shell eggs in a second jar. Cover that egg with corn syrup. Secure the lid and let the jar sit for 72 hours. Record your observations. The egg has changed size and shape.

Conclusion/What is going on? Surfaces that appear solid but actually allow some things to pass through them are called "semi-permeable." Semi-permeable membranes around our cells allow nutrients into the cell and waste products out. This experiment shows the flow of materials through the semi-permeable membrane of an egg. The shell is made from calcium carbonate. It is dissolved by vinegar and releases carbon dioxide gas (bubbles). After the shell is dissolved, the membrane pulls the vinegar inside the egg, making it appear larger. The molecules in the syrup and inside the egg, however, are too large to move out through the membrane.

Report and Present: Write out the steps and what you saw. Explain the results using "What is going on?" above to help you. Display both jars and eggs.

Ant Trails

Hypothesis or Statement of Purpose: To understand scent-based communication.

What you need:

Shoe box	Water
Masking tape	Trowel
Plastic wrap	Gloves
Scissors	Soil sample
Jar and cover	Water
Saucer	Cardboard
Small piece of fruit	

Test, watch, and record: Cut a strip of cardboard the width of the shoebox plus 2 inches and just shorter than the height of the shoebox. Cut a notch close to the edge of the strip from the bottom up about 1 inch. Fold the edge of the strip 1 inch from the edge one direction and fold the other end of the cardboard 1 inch from the edge in the other direction. Place the strip inside the box midway to form a wall. Tape the folded ends to the box. Place a piece fruit on the dish and sprinkle it with sugar and water. Place the dish on one side of the wall in the shoebox. In the garden, lift rocks to find ants. Dig the soil around it and place the ants in a jar. Pour the ants into the side of the box opposite the wall from the fruit. Cover the box with plastic wrap, taped in place. Let sit for 30 minutes. Record your observations.

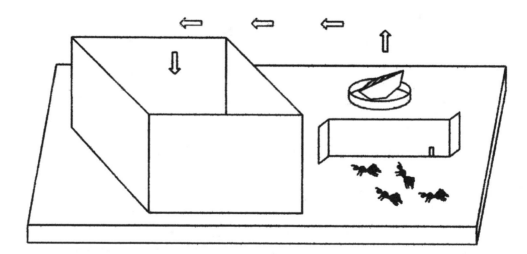

Conclusion/What is going on? The ants explore until one of them finds the fruit. They may go through the notch or over the wall. Ants communicate with each other by scent. As they move, they leave a trail of chemicals called "pheromones." Other ants can follow that scent.

Report and Present: Write out the steps and what you saw. Explain the results using "What is going on?" above to help you. Take photographs or make drawings of the experiment to display.

Water Bugs

Hypothesis or Statement of Purpose: To understand how insects can be supported by surface tension of water.

What you need:

Small piece of metal window screening   Water
Plastic cup   Liquid soap

Test, watch, and record: Bend the sides of a piece of metal window screen upward to make a boat. Fill a cup with water and place the boat on top of the water. Record your observations. Now remove the boat and mix liquid soap into the water. Try floating the boat again. Record your observations.

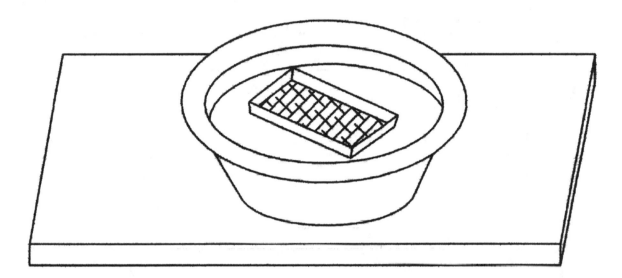

Conclusion/What is going on? Water has a skin, called "surface tension." Even though the boat is metal and filled with holes, it floats on top of the water. Water bugs can skim across the top of water without sinking just like the metal boat can, because the water supports their weight. Also their small weight is spread out over a larger area by their long legs. When soap is added, the boat sinks. Soap weakens the surface tension of the water so that it can no longer hold up the boat.

Report and Present: Write out the steps and what you saw. Explain the results using "What is going on?" above to help you. Display the "bug" and have a bowl of water to show how this works at your presentation.

Spider Sense

Hypothesis or Statement of Purpose: To understand how spiders sense the presence of food.

What you need:

> String
>
> Table
>
> Scissors

Test, watch, and record: Cut a length of string long enough to tie between two table legs. Pluck one end of the string with one hand and gently touch the other end of the string. You should be able to feel the vibrations of the string at the end opposite from the one you pluck. Try plucking gently and firmly. You should be able to sense the strength of the vibrations at the other end. Record your observations.

Conclusion/What is going on? Plucking causes the entire string to vibrate. A harder plucking causes more vibration. When a creature lands in a spider web, the threads vibrate. The spider feels the vibration through hairs on its legs and knows food is there. If the creature is too large for the spider, the threads will vibrate more. If the creature is too small to bother with, the threads will vibrate less.

Report and Present: Write out the steps and what you saw. Explain the results using "What is going on?" above to help you. Tie the string between two legs of your display table and let other students recreate the experiment.

PLANTS

Chlorophyll in Plants

Hypothesis or Statement of Purpose: To understand the importance of sunlight on plant survival.

What you need:

>A green houseplant   Scissors
>Black paper   Tape

Test, watch, and record: Cut a piece of paper and wrap it around one leaf of a houseplant. Tape the paper together to keep light from reaching the leaf. Set the plant in sunlight for 7–10 days. Uncover the leaf. Record your observations.

Conclusion/What is going on? The covered leaf should be lighter in color than the other leaves. The plant contains a chemical called "chlorophyll" that gives the leaf its green color. Without sunlight, this green color is not produced.

Report and Present: Write out the steps and what you saw. Explain the results using "What is going on?" above to help you. Display your plant.

From Carol Peterson, *Jump into Science: Themed Science Fairs*. Westport, CT: Teacher Ideas Press. © 2007 by Carol Peterson.

Capillaries

Hypothesis or Statement of Purpose: To understand capillary action in plants.

What you need:

Three tall drinking glasses	Blue food coloring
Water	Scissors
Stalk of celery with leaves	Spoon
Red food coloring	

Test, watch, and record: Fill two glasses half full of water. Add 6 to 8 drops of red food coloring to one glass and stir. Add 6 to 8 drops of blue food coloring to the second glass and stir. With scissors, split the celery stalk lengthwise into two sections, leaving it attached at the top. Place one section into each glass. Place a separate celery stalk into an empty glass. Let all three glasses sit overnight. Record your observations.

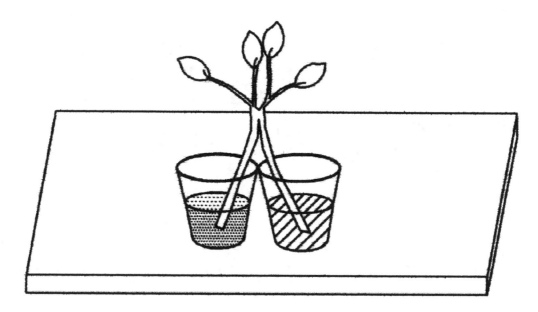

Conclusion/What is going on? The stalk draws colored water up through it because of "capillary action"—the ability of a liquid to climb through small spaces. This is important to plants because they draw liquid and nutrients from the soil up through the roots and out to the ends of leaves. The celery in the empty glass is limp because it has lost water. If you add water to the glass, the celery will absorb it via capillary action and become stiff again after a few hours.

Report and Present: Write out the steps and what you saw. Explain the results using "What is going on?" above to help you. Display your celery stalks or photographs or drawings of them.

Plant Pigments

Hypothesis or Statement of Purpose: To understand how pigment affects photosynthesis.

What you need:

1 cup chopped spinach leaves	Four glass cups
1 cup chopped parsley	Cooking pot
1 cup chopped coleus leaves	Labels
Red food coloring	Four paper clips
Blue food coloring	Tablespoon
Yellow food coloring	1 cup measure
Paper towels	Water
Rubbing alcohol	

Test, watch, and record: Place 1 cup of water and 20 drops of each food coloring in a pan and boil for 10 minutes. Allow the water to cool. Pour the mixture into a cup and add 4 tablespoons of alcohol. Label the cup "1." This is the control solution. Wash the pan. Fill it with 1 cup water and the spinach. Boil for 10 minutes and cool. Pour into a second cup labeled "2." Add 4 tablespoons alcohol. Wash the pan and repeat the steps for the parsley (cup 3) and coleus (cup 4).

Cut the paper towel into four 1-inch-wide strips and label them "1," "2," "3," and "4." Place one strip into its matching numbered cup so only the bottom of the paper touches the liquid. Attach the paper towel with a paper clip to the side of the cup so it doesn't fall in. Let each paper sit for 30 minutes. Observe the liquid seep up the paper. After 30 minutes, remove the papers and place them on a paper towel to dry. Record your observations. Which plant contained the most pigment?

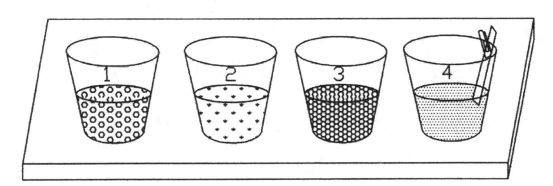

Conclusion/What is going on? Chlorophyll is the green pigment that gives leaves their color. Chlorophyll absorbs light from the sun and stores it to form sugar and oxygen (its own food) out of carbon dioxide in the air and water from soil. The process is called "photosynthesis." Pigments appear to our eye as color because of the wavelengths of light they reflect. Many pigments are present within the plant cell. The different pigments allow the plant to absorb different light wavelengths. Green chlorophyll breaks down faster than other pigments so in autumn, green leaves change color to yellow and orange.

Report and Present: Write out the steps and what you saw. Explain the results using "What is going on?" above to help you. Display your paper strips and samples of the original plants.

From Carol Peterson, *Jump into Science: Themed Science Fairs.* Westport, CT: Teacher Ideas Press. © 2007 by Carol Peterson.

Bean Seeds

Hypothesis or Statement of Purpose: To understand how seeds grow from a resting stage.

What you need:

A dozen dry beans   Small jar with lid
Water   Paper towel

Test, watch, and record: Observe a dried bean and locate the micropyle, hilum, and coat. Make a drawing of the bean and label its parts. Place the dried beans in the jar. Fill the jar with water and screw on the lid. Let it sit overnight. Drain off the water and place the beans on the paper towel. With your fingernails, remove the outer layer and open several of the softened beans. Observe and record what is inside. Try altering this experiment by planting one of the unopened bean seeds in fertile soil. Water it and place in sun. Care for the seed and see if it grows. Record observations through the growing cycle. Locate each part of the bean and understand its function. Make a drawing of the bean parts and label them.

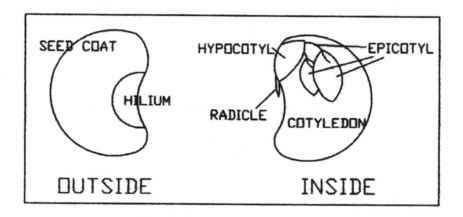

Conclusion/What is going on? Germination is how some plants grow seeds or beans from a resting stage. Try to find the following parts of the bean.

Seed coat—protective covering (outside)

Cotyledon—food for the growing plant (inside)

Hilum—the place where the bean was attached to the plant (outside)

Epicotyl—the upper end contains the "plumules," which form the leaves; the lower end becomes part of the stem (inside)

Hypocotyl—forms the stem of the bean plant (inside)

Radicle—forms the roots of the bean (inside)

Report and Present: Write out the steps and what you saw. Explain the results using "What is going on?" above to help you. Display your chart of the bean parts.

How Fruit Ripens

Hypothesis or Statement of Purpose: To understand how fruit ripens.

What you need:

Two very ripe bananas

Three green bananas

Two unripe fruit of another kind, such as avocado, apple, peach, or kiwi

Three brown paper bags

Stapler

Marking pen

Test, watch, and record: Label a bag "1" and it place one green banana inside. Label a second bag "2" and place one green banana and one ripe banana inside. Label a third bag "3" and place one unripe fruit and one ripe banana inside. Fold down the ends of the three bags and staple them closed. Set the bags, the extra green banana, and the other unripe fruit on the counter for 5 days. Make sure the unbagged fruit is not near each other. After 5 days, open the bags and compare all 7 pieces of fruit for ripeness. Cut open if necessary. Record your observations.

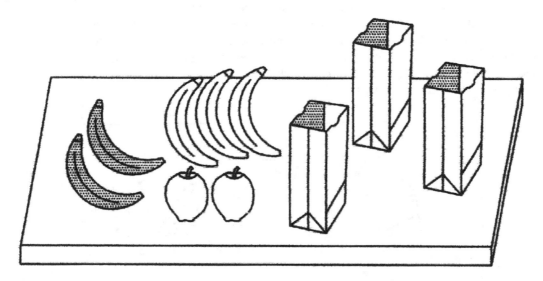

Conclusion/What is going on? The fruit left on the counter and the banana in bag 1 may show some ripening. The bananas in bag 2 and the fruit and banana in bag 3 should be very ripe. As fruit ripens, it takes in oxygen and gives off carbon dioxide and another gas called "ethylene." Ethylene speeds the ripening of other fruit nearby. So if two fruit are together in a bag, the ethylene stays in the bag. If there is a single fruit in the bag, the fruit makes its own ethylene but does not get any from other fruit. In the open air, air currents carry ethylene away so fruit ripens less. Fruit packagers often gas fruit with ethylene to ripen it quickly. That is harmless to people's health, but fruit may taste sweeter if it ripens slowly.

Report and Present: Write out the steps and what you saw. Explain the results using "What is going on?" above to help you. Display drawings or photos. Display the fruit if it has not rotted.

From Carol Peterson, *Jump into Science: Themed Science Fairs*. Westport, CT: Teacher Ideas Press.
© 2007 by Carol Peterson.

Leaf Veins

Hypothesis or Statement of Purpose: To understand the structure of leaves.

What you need:

Different types of leaves	Small rock
Medium-sized pan	Paper towels
Bowl	Wax paper
Baking soda	Several books
Water	Bleach
Spoon	Tongs
Measuring spoon	Several sheets of black paper
Measuring cup	

Test, watch, and record: Gather several types of leaves. In a pan, mix 1 teaspoon baking soda and 2 cups water. Add leaves and place a small rock on top to keep the leaves underwater. Put pan in sun for 2 weeks. Carefully remove the leaves and rinse them in a bowl of water. Place them on a paper towel to dry. When dry, place them between wax paper and set a book on top. After a few days remove books and paper. Mix a ½ cup bleach and 2 cups water in bowl. One at a time, place each leaf in the bleach water. When the leaf turns white, remove it with tongs and place it on a paper towel to dry. Mount on black paper. Record your observations about each leaf.

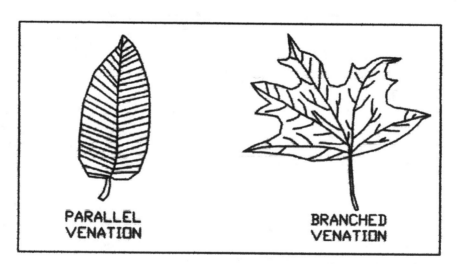

PARALLEL VENATION

BRANCHED VENATION

Conclusion/What is going on? You can see the structure of the leaf's veins, called "venation." Some veins run next to each other, like stripes, called "parallel venation." Other leaves have veins that are thick at the stem and fan out thinner at the edge, called "branched venation."

Report and Present: Write out the steps and what you saw. Compare the structure of the veins and label each as parallel or branched venation. Try to find examples of both types of venation. If you can, find out which type of tree or bush each leaf is from and label it. Take photos of the tree or bush from which the leaf was taken. Display leaves.

 From Carol Peterson, *Jump into Science: Themed Science Fairs*. Westport, CT: Teacher Ideas Press. © 2007 by Carol Peterson.

Natural Dyes

Hypothesis or Statement of Purpose: To understand ways plant pigment can be used.

What you need:

- 18–20 inches of white cotton cloth
- 18–20 inches of synthetic cloth (nylon or polyester)
- Scissors
- 4 plastic cups
- Tablespoon
- Knife
- Hammer
- Cutting board
- Eight zippered plastic bags
- Permanent black marker
- 2 cups red cabbage
- 2 cups fresh carrots
- 2 cups fresh or frozen blueberries
- 2 cups canned beets
- Can opener
- Paper towels
- Paper

Test, watch, and record: With scissors, cut four pieces of each type of cloth into 3- to 4-inch squares. With the marker, mark "C" on each piece of cotton cloth and "S" on each piece of synthetic cloth. Label each cup with the name of one of the foods you are using. With the knife and cutting board, carefully cut each food into small pieces and put them into separate small plastic bags. Place one bag at a time on a cutting board and mash the food with a hammer, being careful not to tear the bag. Empty the mashed food into the cup with that food's label. Add 2 tablespoons of water to each cup and stir. Place 1 piece of each of the two types of cloth into each cup and stir to make sure they are wet. Let sit overnight. Rinse each cloth and set it on a paper towel in front of the labeled cup. Record which food and cloth resulted in the deepest color.

Conclusion/What is going on? You should find that the cotton cloth accepted the color better. This is because the synthetic cloth is made from fibers that do not absorb liquid.

Report and Present: Write out the steps and what you saw. Explain the results using "What is going on?" above to help you. Create a chart where you can label and display the samples by type of dye and fabric.

From Carol Peterson, *Jump into Science: Themed Science Fairs.* Westport, CT: Teacher Ideas Press. © 2007 by Carol Peterson.

Perfume

Hypothesis or Statement of Purpose: To understand our sense of smell and the pleasing scent of plants.

What you need:

Small jars with lids
Rubbing alcohol
Spoon
Cotton swabs, one for each sample
Fork
Paper towels

Tablespoon measurer
Bottom half of egg carton
Masking tape
Marking pen
Fresh or dried blossoms, leaves and spices such as rose
    petals, small blossoms, eucalyptus leaves, pine
    needles, mint, whole cloves

Test, watch, and record: Place some of each plant into its own jar. Label the jar with the plant name, using the tape and marker. Crush the plant slightly against the side of the jar with a spoon. (You will not be able to crush the cloves.) Add 4 tablespoons of rubbing alcohol to each jar. Attach the lids securely and shake the jars. Put jars in a warm place for 7 days. Label spaces on an egg carton, allowing 2 cups for each plant. After 7 days, open each jar one at a time, and dip a swab into the liquid. Record its smell. Let the swab dry for 5 minutes and record its smell again. Tape the swab in the eggcup above its label. With the fork, remove a sample of the plant from each jar and set it on a paper towel to drain. Smell the plant sample and write a description of the smell. Let the plant dry overnight and then tape it to the eggcup next to the swab.

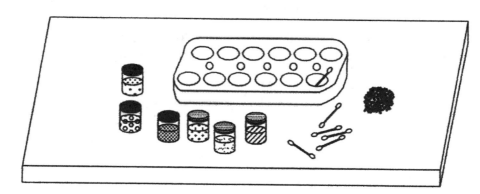

Conclusion/What is going on? Alcohol removes the oil from the plant. The wet swab will smell of alcohol. When dry, the swab will smell like the plant because the alcohol has evaporated, leaving the scented oil. The dried plant will have little smell because the scent has transferred from it to the liquid.

Report and Present: Write out the steps and what you saw. Explain the results using "What is going on?" above to help you. Display the chart, the jars, and the egg carton. Have swabs for others to test the scent. Display the original plant, and if you can, include a photo or drawing as the plant appears in nature.

From Carol Peterson, *Jump into Science: Themed Science Fairs*. Westport, CT: Teacher Ideas Press.
© 2007 by Carol Peterson.

Plant Cuttings

Hypothesis or Statement of Purpose: To understand how to grow a plant from a cutting.

What you need:

Ivy	Jar or drinking glass
Scissors	Water

Test, watch, and record: Cut a length of ivy about 6 inches long. Stick the cut end into a glass of water and set it in a sunny place for 7 days. Record your observations.

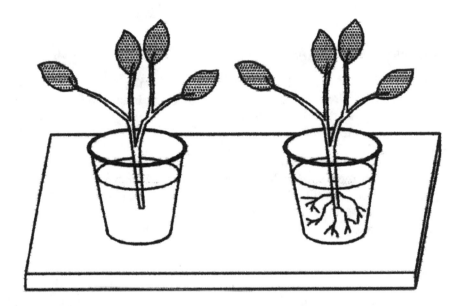

Conclusion/What is going on? Tiny roots will start to grow from the bottom of the cut stem. This is one way new plants can be grown from some plants rather than through seeds.

Report and Present: Write out the steps and what you saw. Explain the results using "What is going on?" above to help you. Display the rooted ivy.

From Carol Peterson, *Jump into Science: Themed Science Fairs.* Westport, CT: Teacher Ideas Press. © 2007 by Carol Peterson.

Plants Grown in Different Colored Light

Hypothesis or Statement of Purpose: To understand how the color of light affects plant growth.

What you need:

Four boxes, 24-inch square and open on one side

Foil

Four light fixtures with 40-watt bulbs

Four plastic filters, 12-inch square, such as cellophane in clear, green, blue, and red

Black plastic cut from garbage bag

Four plastic cups

Potting soil

40 bean seeds of one type

Water

Spray bottle

Note: This experiment requires 2 months.

Test, watch, and record: Hypothesize which color of light will make plants grow best or whether there will be no difference. Set up four boxes the same way. Cut a hole in the top of each box about 10 inches square. Line boxes with foil and tape the foil in place. Set boxes so the opening is to the front. Drape black plastic over the front and secure with tape. Tape a sheet of colored cellophane over the top hole on each box. Set a light 12 inches above each hole.

Pour 3 inches of potting soil in each cup. Place 10 seeds in each cup, spaced equally. Cover with a ½ inch of soil and water carefully. Place one cup into each box. Turn on the lights for 8 to 10 hours a day. Check the soil daily and spray with water if needed. Record your observations daily. After the seeds sprout, measure and record the growth daily for 1 month.

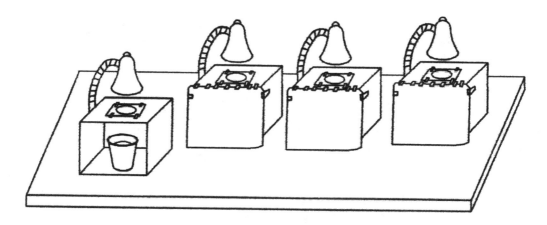

Conclusion/What is going on? Different pigments react to light differently. Each pigment absorbs all colors of light except the color of the pigment. Green pigment is most important for photosynthesis. So if a green plant is grown under green light it will reflect most of the light instead of absorbing it. Because the plant cannot perform photosynthesis, it starves.

Report and Present: Write out the steps and what you saw. Explain the results using "What is going on?" above to help you. Display your plants, labeled according to which color light it received.

Spores

Hypothesis or Statement of Purpose: To understand mold and spores.

What you need:

> Several fresh mushrooms that have begun to open on the underside
>
> Two sheets of black construction paper
>
> Two large bowls

Test, watch, and record: Use edible mushrooms to avoid handling ones that might be poisonous. Remove stems so the undersides lay flat. Set half of them round side up on each piece of construction paper. Cover each set of mushrooms with a bowl and set in a cool place. After a few hours, remove the bowl from one set of mushrooms. Let the other set of mushrooms rest for 3 days. Then remove the second bowl and the mushrooms. Compare both sets of paper and record your observations.

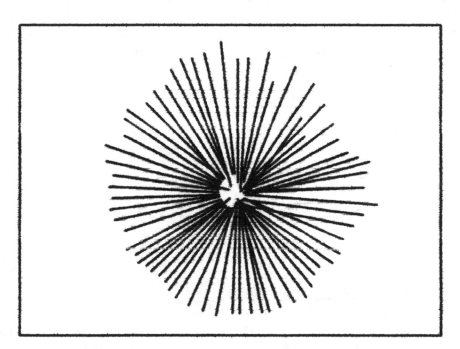

Conclusion/What is going on? The underside of mushrooms contains "spores." When mushrooms are growing, these spores fall off and land in soil to grow new mushrooms. The patterns on the paper are spores from the mushrooms.

Report and Present: Write out the steps and what you saw. Explain the results using "What is going on?" above to help you. Display your papers.

HUMANS

Fingerprints

Hypothesis or Statement of Purpose: To understand fingerprints and how to make them.

What you need:

    2 sheets of white paper

    Sharpened pencil

    Transparent tape

Test, watch, and record: On a sheet of paper, create 10 spaces and label them "Right Hand 1–5" and "Left Hand 1–5." Rub the pencil on the second sheet of paper to leave a layer of pencil lead on the paper. Rub your thumb across the pencil lead. Cut off about 2 inches of tape. Press your lead-covered finger onto the sticky side of the tape. Place the tape, sticky-side down, onto a second sheet of white paper above the "1" space for that hand. Repeat with all fingers. Observe each finger and its print and record your observations.

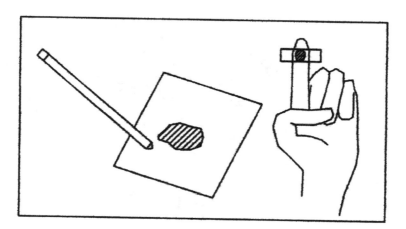

Conclusion/What is going on? The fingerprint and the pattern on the finger it came from are the same. The inner layer of skin has tiny projections. The outer skin follows those projections and causes a pattern. Each person has different fingerprints, which never change from birth across the life span. Also the fingerprints from each finger on the same person are different. Because each person has unique fingerprints, police often use fingerprinting to determine who might have committed a crime. There are different methods of taking fingerprints depending on the surface where the fingerprint is found. For example, police might use carbon or charcoal powder to show prints on surfaces such as glass or plastic. On porous things such as paper or cloth, however, police might use an iodine vapor. On those surfaces, oil and perspiration from fingers spread out, and powder may not always leave an accurate print.

Report and Present: Write out the steps and what you saw. Explain the results using "What is going on?" above to help you. Have extra paper, tape, and pencils available so that students can study their own fingerprints

From Carol Peterson, *Jump into Science: Themed Science Fairs*. Westport, CT: Teacher Ideas Press. © 2007 by Carol Peterson.

Calcium in Bones

Hypothesis or Statement of Purpose: To understand the importance of calcium in bones.

What you need:

Two large jars the same size

Two cooked chicken bones the same size (such as two drumsticks, with meat removed and the bone then washed)

Measuring cup

White vinegar

Water

Two labels

Marking pen

Tongs

Paper towels

Test, watch, and record: Measure water into one of the jars. Label that jar "water." Measure the same amount of vinegar into the second jar. Place one bone in each jar and set the jars in the sun for 7 days. With tongs, remove the bones and let them dry on paper towels. Observe the feel and appearance of the bones and how they react to pressure. Record your observations.

Conclusion/What is going on? The bone in vinegar can be easily bent. The bone in water is unchanged. Bones contain calcium, a mineral that makes bones strong. Vinegar is an acid and dissolves calcium in the bone. Without calcium, the bone became soft.

Report and Present: Write out the steps and what you saw. Explain the results using "What is going on?" above to help you. Display both bones. Find out and report what foods contain high levels of calcium. Report the amount of calcium children and adults should eat daily for bone health.

Our Camera

Hypothesis or Statement of Purpose: To understand how our eye lens is like a camera.

What you need:

Paper towel tube

Test, watch, and record: Hold one end of an empty paper towel tube against one eye. Keep both eyes open. Look through the tube at an object across the room. Place your other hand next to the tube toward the far end of the tube. It should appear that there is a hole through the middle of your hand. Record your observations.

Now look out a window without the tube. Hold up your finger at arm's length away. Close one eye and look out at an object with the other eye, just above your finger. Make a note of the objects you see. Now, keeping your position, including your finger up, close that eye and open the other. You should see that the objects in your field of vision have shifted.

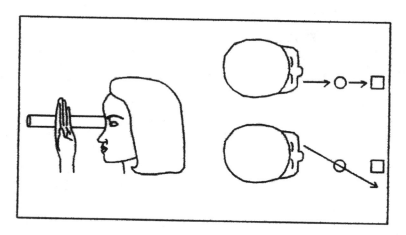

Conclusion/What is going on? Our eyes are like cameras with lenses that form images. Our eye can also adjust the amount of light inside through the pupil. And our eye can register an image as light and dark, just like a camera does onto film. The image in our eyes is registered through nerves on the retina (the back of the eye). Each nerve is like a wire to the brain. When light hits the nerve on the retina, a signal travels to the brain. There messages from other nerves on the retina form a pattern. The brain can then recognize the object. In the first experiment, the eye that looked through the tube did not see your hand. The eye that saw your hand did not see the end of the tube. Because your brain put the two together at the same time, you saw a hole in your hand. The second experiment shows how each eye sees different images because each eye is in a different place on your head. Your brain must put the 2 images together to form an idea of what you're looking at. This ability helps the brain judge distances.

Report and Present: Write out the steps and what you saw. Explain the results using "What is going on?" above to help you. Make a drawing of the eye and label its parts. Have the tube for other students to try.

Extent of Vision

Hypothesis or Statement of Purpose: To understand dominant eye and peripheral vision.

What you need:

Two pieces of cardboard about 6 inches square

Chair

A friend

Test, watch, and record: To check your dominant eye, hold your hands out in front of you with your arms extended. Form a triangle between your hands. As you look through and at an object out the other side of the triangle, bring your hands up to your face. Note which eye your triangle is in front of. That eye is your dominant eye. Have your friend do this experiment. Note whether you both had the same dominant eye or different ones.

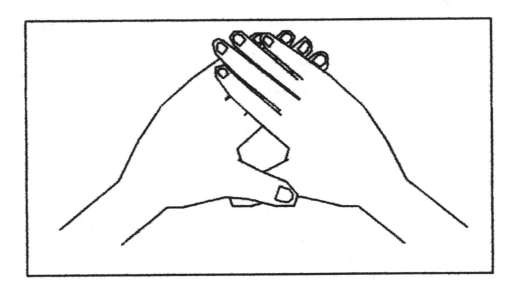

Now have your friend sit on a chair. Stand behind him or her and hold one card in each hand near your friend's ear. Have him or her look straight ahead. Slowly bring the cards around and forward, and ask your friend to tell you to stop when he or she can first see them. Note where the cards are when your friend can first see them. Switch places and have your friend hold the cards for you.

Conclusion/What is going on? Both eyes send messages to your brain telling it what it sees. One eye, however, is called "dominant" because the brain receives stronger messages from that eye rather than the other. Peripheral vision is the ability of your eyes to see objects on your side even if you are looking ahead.

Report and Present: Write out the steps and what you observed. Explain the results, using "What is going on?" above to help you.

Optical Illusions

Hypothesis or Statement of Purpose: To understand how optical illusions fool our brain.

What you need:

> Photocopies of optical illusions
> Lamp with incandescent lightbulb

Test, watch, and record: Look at each of the drawings. In figure 1, which of the two lines appear longer? In figure 2, are the center lines straight or curved? Move figure 3 in a circle. Do the circles continue to move after you stop rotating them? Turn on the lamp and stare at the lightbulb for 30 seconds. Then close your eyes. What do you see? Record your observations.

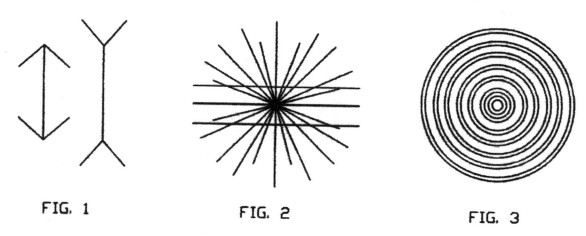

FIG. 1   FIG. 2   FIG. 3

Conclusion/What is going on? In figure 1, the parallel lines are equal. In figure 2, the center lines are straight. Figure 3 shows "persistence of vision," which means the circles appear to move after it has stopped. When you closed your eyes after looking at the lightbulb, you "see" a dark spot. This is called an "after image"—the reverse of the image is temporarily "burned" into the nerve endings of your retina, and the image stays for a while.

Report and Present: Write out the steps and what you saw. Explain the results using "What is going on?" above to help you. Have pictures at the presentation for other students to try.

Vision and Color

Hypothesis or Statement of Purpose: To understand the way our eye sees colors.

What you need:

Jar lid 2 to 3 inches in diameter	Blue felt marker
Pencil	Green felt marker
Scissors	Sharp nail
Ruler	Thin cardboard or poster board 4 inches by 4 inches
Red felt marker	

Test, watch, and record: Use the lid to trace a circle on cardboard. Divide the circle into three equal parts. Make each part a different color. Poke a nail through the center of the circle and slide a pencil through, pointed end down. Spin the circle on a flat surface like a top. Record your observations.

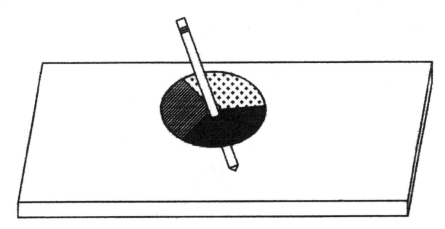

Conclusion/What is going on? The back of the eye has an area called the "retina." In the retina are three "cones." Each cone can sense either red, blue, or green. When you look at something green, only the green cones receive green light. They send a message to your brain telling it that you see green. When the same number of blue and red cones receive light, they combine to tell you that you are seeing purple. As this circle spins, the cones in your retina receive light to the red, green, and blue cones at the same time. They combine to tell your brain that you are seeing the color white.

Report and Present: Write out the steps and what you observed. Explain the results, using "What is going on?" above to help you. Draw a diagram of the human eye, including the retina and cones. Display it along with your color wheel.

Taste Buds

Hypothesis or Statement of Purpose: To understand the location of taste buds.

What you need:

Toothpicks	Paper
Sugar	Pencil
Vinegar	Small paper cups
Salt	Tablespoon
Lemon juice	Water
Chopped onion	

Test, watch, and record: Draw an oval on a piece of paper. Label one end "tip" and the other end "back." In each of the paper cups, place 1 tablespoon of each food. Add 1 tablespoon of water to the sugar, the salt, and the onion to create juice. Dip a toothpick into each liquid and place it first on the end of your tongue, then in the middle, then the back, and then the side. Record where on your tongue you can taste each flavor.

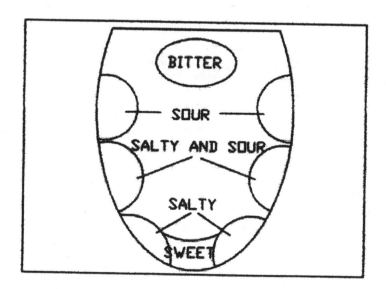

Conclusion/What is going on? Your taste buds are located on your tongue. Different buds are able to sense different tastes. The buds that detect sour flavors such as vinegar and lemon are mainly on the sides of your tongue. Salt is sensed on the tip of your tongue and the side. Sweet flavor is detected on top of the tongue. Bitter flavors such as onion are sensed at the back.

Report and Present: Write out the steps you used in this experiment and what you saw. Explain the results using "What is going on?" above to help you. Let students sample the dips. Make sure they use clean toothpicks for each dip. Provide a basket or cup for used toothpicks. Display your drawing of the tongue with the location of the taste buds.

From Carol Peterson, *Jump into Science: Themed Science Fairs*. Westport, CT: Teacher Ideas Press.
© 2007 by Carol Peterson.

Taste and Smell

Hypothesis or Statement of Purpose: To understand the relationship between taste and smell.

What you need:

Toothpicks   Slice of raw onion
Slice of raw apple, peeled   Slice of raw potato, peeled

Test, watch, and record: Blindfold a friend. Have your friend pinch his or her nose closed. From a toothpick, feed your friend each item. Have him or her guess what he or she is eating without smelling, seeing, or feeling it. Record both your friend's guess and the actual item.

Conclusion/What is going on? Taste and smell are closely related. Each of these foods have similar textures. Without the sense of smell, it is hard to tell the difference in each items' taste.

Report and Present: Write out the steps you used in this experiment and what you saw. Explain the results using "What is going on?" above to help you. Have toothpicks and samples of unlabeled items. (Mark the containers secretly so you know what the items are.) Have students close their eyes, hold their noses, and sample them. Make sure they use clean toothpicks each time. Display a drawing of a tongue with the location of the taste buds.

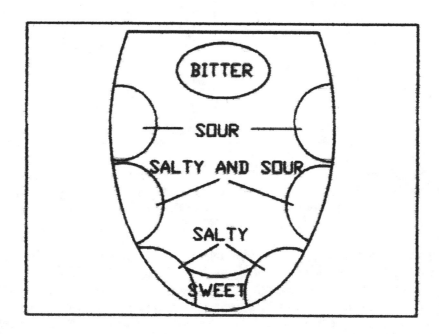

Muscles

Hypothesis or Statement of Purpose: To understand how muscles move by seeing the relationships between muscle sets.

What you need:

Heavy cardboard

Three brass paper fasteners

Sharp nail

Two thin rubber bands, 3 to 4 inches long

Strip of paper 2 inches by 6 inches

Tape

Scissors

Test, watch, and record: Cut two strips of cardboard 1 inch by 4 inches. With a nail, poke a hole in one end of each strip. Join the strips with a fastener through both holes. Then poke a nail through the other ends of the strips. Place one end of each rubber band over the hole. Slide a fastener through them and into each hole to secure the rubber bands. Wrap a strip of paper several times around the joint and tape in place so the rubber bands will not slip off when the joint is bent. Bend and open the cardboard strips at the joint and observe the rubber bands.

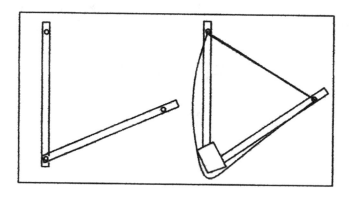

Now extend your arm in front of you. Have a friend measure around your upper arm at the largest place. Record that measurement. Now contract your muscle, by bringing your hand up toward your head, while leaving your upper arm in the same position. Have your friend measure your arm at the same point. Record and compare both measurements.

Conclusion/What is going on? To move parts of your body, muscles must work in pairs. One muscle, called the "extensor" becomes longer (extends) to straighten a body part out. The other muscle, called the "flexor," pulls up (contracts) to bend a joint upward. The two strips represent the upper and lower bones in an arm. The rubber bands represent the muscles. When the cardboard "arm" is bent, the rubber band "muscle" on the inside of the bend relaxes, while the outside rubber band "muscle" stretches. When the arm is straightened, the inside muscle stretches, and the outside muscle relaxes. The measurement when the arm is extended is less than when it is flexed because the muscle is stretched thinner.

Report and Present: Write out the steps and what you observed. Explain the results, using "What is going on?" above to help you. Display your arm model. Have a tape measure for students to measure their muscles while flexed and extended.

Heart Rate

Hypothesis or Statement of Purpose: To understand heart rate.

What you need:

    Two funnels

    1 to 2 feet of plastic tubing

    Watch with a second hand

Test, watch, and record: Slide one end of the tube over the narrow end of the funnels. Place one funnel over your heart and one around your ear. Listen for your heart beat. Take a deep breath and listen to the air going to and from your lungs. Record what you hear.

Find your heartbeat by locating your pulse either at your wrist or along the side of your neck just behind and below your ear. Press firmly but gently with your fingers. Do not use your thumb, because your thumb also has a pulse. When you can feel your heartbeat, look at your watch. When the second hand is at the "12," begin counting your heartbeats. Continue counting until the second hand on the watch reaches the "3." Multiply that number by four. That figure is the number of times your heart beats in 1 minute (called your "heart rate") .

Now run in place for 2 minutes. Find your pulse again and record your heart rate. Sit down for 10 minutes. Check and record your heart rate again. Wait another 10 minutes and check and record your heart rate again. Check the resting heart rate of people who are much larger than you are and much smaller. What can you hypothesize about how size affects heart rate?

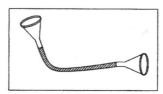

Conclusion/What is going on? The funnel and tube form a simple stethoscope. The heart is a strong muscle with four chambers. One chamber receives blood from the body that has no oxygen in it. It pumps the blood to a second chamber, which sends it to the lungs. A third chamber receives blood back from the lungs now rich with oxygen. That chamber sends it to the fourth chamber, which pumps it out to the body. The heartbeat is the sound the heart makes as it pumps. The air sound is oxygen breathed in through your mouth or nose, entering the airway, and going to the lungs.

You should have found that your heart rate became faster after you ran. This is because the heart must work harder to get oxygen to parts of your body when you need it for extra activity. It then takes the heart time to slow down and return to its normal pace. As a general rule, the smaller someone is, the faster his or her heart rate because a smaller heart must work faster to get the blood where it needs to go. A person, who has trained athletically may have a very slow heart rate because the training has strengthened the heart muscle to work better.

Report and Present: Write out the steps and what you observed. Explain the results, using "What is going on?" above to help you. Display your stethoscope and record of heart rates. Have other students test their own heart rate. Find who has the fastest and slowest heart rates.

Touch and Feeling

Hypothesis or Statement of Purpose: To understand our sense of touch.

What you need:

> Two pencils   Water
> Blindfold   Friend

Test, watch, and record: Blindfold a friend. Have him cross his fingers. Touch ONE sharp pencil to the insides of the two fingers. Ask him how many pencils he feels. While he is still blindfolded, hold the TWO pencils together and touch them against the back of his neck. Ask him how many pencils he feels. Record his responses. Now rub a bit of water onto the back of your hand. Blow on your hand. Observe and record how your hand feels.

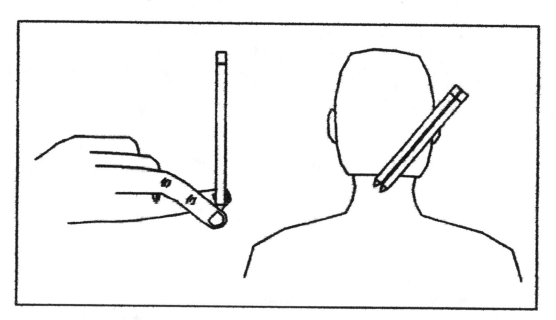

Conclusion/What is going on? Your blindfolded friend should think there are two pencils when you touched one to his crossed fingers. This is because normally the opposite sides of those same fingers are next to each other and are in a different position. When you touched the two pencils to the back of his neck, he felt them as one point. This is because our sense of touch is less sensitive on the back of our neck, where it is less needed. When you blew your warm breath across your wet hand, it felt cool. Your breath caused the water to evaporate. Evaporation (into clouds) is one way heat moves from one place on Earth to another. Our body stays cool by producing sweat. Sweat then evaporates and removes some our body's heat.

Report and Present: Write out the steps and what you observed. Explain the results, using "What is going on?" above to help you. Create diagrams of your experiment and display them.

PHYSICAL SCIENCE UNIT

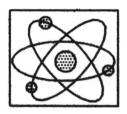

Chemistry

Simple Machines

Physical Forces

Behavior of Physical Laws

CHEMISTRY

Hypothesis or Statement of Purpose: To identify physical and chemical reactions.

What you need:

Two plastic cups   Vegetable oil
Water   Food coloring
Measuring cup   Sugar
Measuring spoons   Two glass bowls
Baking soda   Spoon
Vinegar   Bleach
One clear plastic soda bottle with cap   4-inch-square piece of blue denim

Test, watch, and record: Observe and record your observations after each step: 1) Place 1 teaspoon baking soda in 2 cups. Add 1 tablespoon vinegar to one cup and 1 tablespoon water to the second cup. 2) Fill a soda bottle halfway with water. Add 2 to 3 drops of food coloring and observe. 3) Add 1 cup vegetable oil to the colored water, cap, and shake. Allow bottle to sit and observe. 4) Stir 3 teaspoons sugar and 1/8 cup water in bowl. Let sit for 2 days until water evaporates. 5) Fill a bowl halfway with bleach. Be careful not to get bleach on clothing. Add denim. Let sit 10 minutes, then rinse.

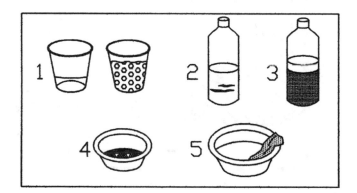

Conclusion/What is going on? In physical reactions, objects may change shape as a result of forces such as motion, temperature, and pressure. In chemical reactions, molecules are changed and a new substance is formed. This change may involve a new color or be evidenced by bubbles. Record observations in a data table. Explain your reasoning about which experiments you think are chemical reactions and which are physical reactions.

Report and Present: Write out the steps and what you saw. Explain the results using "What is going on?" above to help you. Include the before and after of some of the items, such as the bleached and unbleached denim, or a new Styrofoam cup and the one from the experiment.

From Carol Peterson, *Jump into Science: Themed Science Fairs.* Westport, CT: Teacher Ideas Press. © 2007 by Carol Peterson.

Density

Hypothesis or Statement of Purpose: To understand how liquids and objects act, based on density.

What you need:

Corn syrup
Large jar
Cooking oil
Red, blue, or green food coloring
Water

Spoon
Cup measurer
Items of different weights such as a metal washer, a cork, a grape, small erasers, a wad of paper, a pebble, a piece of food

Test, watch, and record: Pour 1 cup corn syrup into the jar. Add 1 cup oil. Rinse cup and fill with water. Add 4 to 5 drops of food coloring. Stir and pour into the jar. Leave the jar undisturbed and observe the liquids. Now record your guess as to whether each of your items will fall through the liquid quickly or slowly, or whether it will float. Then drop each item. Record how it falls within the liquid, including its speed and whether your guess was correct.

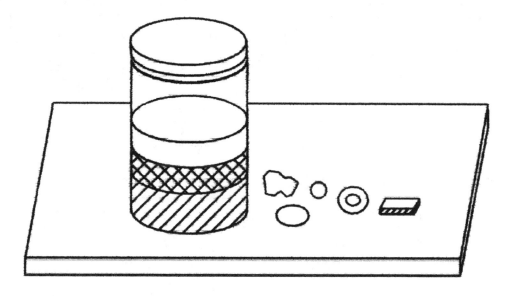

Conclusion/What is going on? Corn syrup is dense and sinks to the bottom of the jar. The oil is less dense than syrup but denser than water so it forms a layer in the middle. The water is least dense and rises to the top. Items such as a metal washer or pebble are heavy and dense and fall through the liquid quickest. Items such as grapes are lighter and less dense, and so they fall slower. Cork and paper are lightest and least dense because they are full of air. They float.

Report and Present: Write out the steps and what you saw. Explain the results using "What is going on?" above to help you. Display your bottle and items.

Solutions and Suspensions

Hypothesis or Statement of Purpose: To understand solutions and suspensions.

What you need:

Two clean plastic soda bottles with caps   Measuring cup
Water   Labels
Teaspoon   Marking pen
Funnel   Leveler such as a table knife with a flat edge or a
Sugar   craft stick
Fine sand

Test, watch, and record: Solutions mix with water and dissolve. Suspensions do not dissolve in water—instead the particles scatter. Guess before you test them whether you think these will be solutions or suspensions. Compare your guess with your observations. Label one bottle "sugar" and one bottle "sand." Remove the caps. Using the funnel, pour ½ cup water into each bottle. Pour a level teaspoonful sugar through the funnel into the bottle labeled "sugar." Pour a level teaspoonful of sand into the bottle labeled "sand." Replace the caps and shake each bottle 10 times. Record your observations.

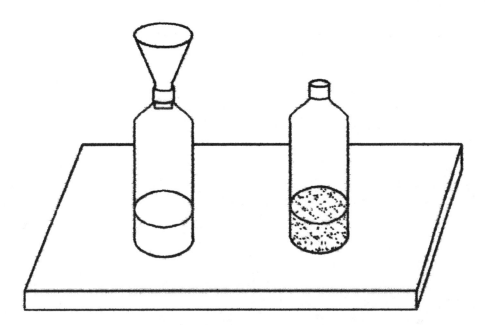

Conclusion/What is going on? The sugar dissolved and made a solution. The sand did not dissolve. It remained suspended in the water. Blood is both a solution and a suspension. The red and white cells in blood do not dissolve. The plasma part of blood is a clear liquid. It contains minerals and nutrients that dissolve. So blood is both a suspension (cells) and solution (plasma).

Report and Present: Write out the steps and what you saw. Explain the results using "What is going on?" above to help you. Display your bottles.

From Carol Peterson, *Jump into Science: Themed Science Fairs*. Westport, CT: Teacher Ideas Press.
© 2007 by Carol Peterson.

Saturated Solutions

Hypothesis or Statement of Purpose: To understand how different substances saturate water.

What you need:

Three clear cups	Baking soda
Water	Salt
Measuring cup	Sugar
Labels	Six teaspoons
Pen	

Test, watch, and record: Fill each cup with ½ cup water. Place one spoon in each cup. Label cups "Soda," "Salt," and "Sugar." Using a separate spoon, add one teaspoon of each item to its glass and stir. Continue to add more of each item to its cup until no more will dissolve. Record the number of teaspoons you added of each item.

Conclusion/What is going on? A saturated solution occurs when a liquid cannot dissolve any more solid. The amount to reach saturation is different for each substance. Create a data table showing which substance was most soluble (the water was able to dissolve more of it) and which was least soluble.

Report and Present: Write out the steps and what you saw. Explain the results using "What is going on?" above to help you. Display your data table.

Tarnish

Hypothesis or Statement of Purpose: To understand how metals combine and break down chemically.

What you need:

Baking soda

Boiling water

Measure cup

Quart measuring cup or large Pyrex bowl

Microwave

Stirring spoon

Potholders or oven mitts

Aluminum foil

Scissors

Piece of tarnished silverware

Paper towel

Test, watch, and record: Measure 4 cups of water into a microwave-proof bowl. Bring water to a boil in the microwave (about 8–10 minutes). While the water is heating, cut 3 strips of foil about 1 inch wide and 6 inches long with scissors. Then using potholders, CAREFULLY remove the bowl from the oven and place it on another potholder. Measure and stir ¾ cup baking soda into the water. Place the foil strips and the tarnished silverware in the bowl for a few minutes. Remove the silver, rinse it, and set it on a paper towel to dry. Record your observations.

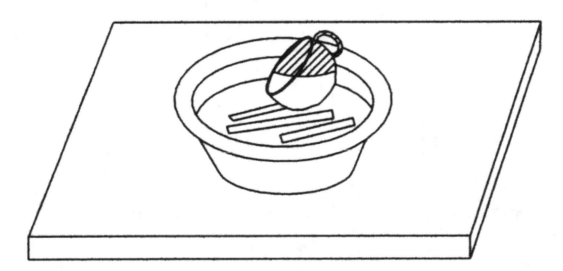

Conclusion/What is going on? Metals are chemically active. This means that the electrons in metals break away and combine with materials outside the metal. Silver combines with oxygen to form a layer of corrosion, called tarnish. The water and soda conduct electricity and allow electrons to pass between the foil and the silver. Heat speeds up the process. Less active metal (the foil) receives electrons from more active metal (silver). So the tarnish is lifted off the silver and deposited onto the foil.

Report and Present: Write out the steps and what you saw. Explain the results using "What is going on?" above to help you. Try dipping the silver only halfway into the water and display the "before and after" piece.

From Carol Peterson, *Jump into Science: Themed Science Fairs.* Westport, CT: Teacher Ideas Press. © 2007 by Carol Peterson.

SIMPLE MACHINES

Inclined Plane

Hypothesis or Statement of Purpose: To understand how an inclined plane works.

What you need:

Table

Piece of cardboard about 4 feet long and
    1 foot wide

Two golf balls or marbles

Masking tape

Test, watch, and record: Set the cardboard against the table and tape one end in place so it forms a ramp. Hold one ball at the top of the ramp and one at the edge of the table. Release both at the same time. Repeat several times, observing the speed and force of the balls as they reach the floor.

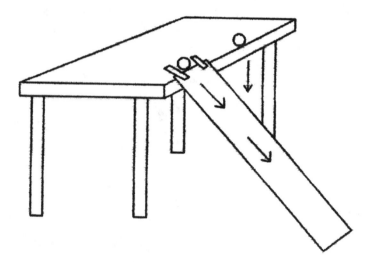

Conclusion/What is going on? In physics, a simple machine is a device that works when only a single force is applied to it. The six simple machines in physics are the inclined plane, pulley, screw, lever, wedge, and wheel and axle. An inclined plane is a flat surface set at an angle against a horizontal surface. It allows you to apply a small force over a longer distance rather than having to use great force. You should find that the ball gains more speed when it travels down the incline than when it falls straight to the ground. This is similar to the way racetracks are banked so that racecars can gain speed. An example of a "virtual" inclined plane is the space shuttle. It enters Earth's atmosphere at an angle to reduce friction. Notice that roads are graded with a slope so water runs away from the center of an intersection to reduce traffic hazards caused by water pooling on the road.

Report and Present: Write out the steps and what you saw. Explain the results using "What is going on?" above to help you. Display your inclined plane. Make a list of ways inclined planes are used in everyday life.

 From Carol Peterson, *Jump into Science: Themed Science Fairs*. Westport, CT: Teacher Ideas Press.

Pulley

Hypothesis or Statement of Purpose: To understand how a pulley works.

What you need:

Heavy wire

Empty spool of thread

Length of string about 4 feet long

Two heavy washers

Test, watch, and record: Thread the wire through the spool of thread and shape the wire into a small coat hanger with a hook. Hook the wire over a clothes rod or hook. Loop the string over the top of the spool. Tie one washer onto the end of each string. Adjust the string so that the washers are balanced. Then pull one washer down and observe what happens to the other. Record your observations. Now remove one of the washers and tie both ends of the string to it. Raise and lower the washer by pulling one side of the string.

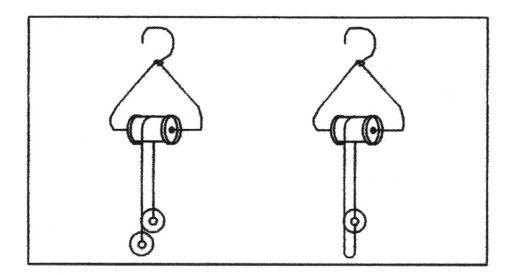

Conclusion/What is going on? In physics, a simple machine is a device that works when only a single force is applied to it. The six simple machines in physics are the inclined plane, pulley, screw, lever, wedge, and wheel and axle. A pulley is one of the six simple machines. It uses a wheel to hold a rope or cable. This design reduces the force needed to lift an object. These are both fixed pulleys, which moves weights in opposite directions. You pull in one direction to move an object in a different direction.

Report and Present: Write out the steps and what you saw. Explain the results using "What is going on?" above to help you. Display your pulley. Make a list of pulleys that are used in everyday life.

Screw

Hypothesis or Statement of Purpose: To understand how a screw acts as a wedge on an inclined plane.

What you need:

A screw	Hammer
Screwdriver	Block of wood
Nail	

Test, watch, and record: Hold a screw in one hand. Place your pointer and thumb fingernails of the other hand inside the ridge of the screw near the point. Turn the screw clockwise. As you turn, the ridges of the screw (called the "thread") begin to spiral down even though your fingers remain in the same place. Finally, the ridges move down so far that the head of the screw reaches your fingers. Now hammer the nail into the block of wood until it is about ½ inch into the wood. Remove the nail by pulling or using the claw end of the hammer. Insert the screw into the nail hole and screw it well into the block of wood with the screwdriver. Observe the threads as they go into the wood.

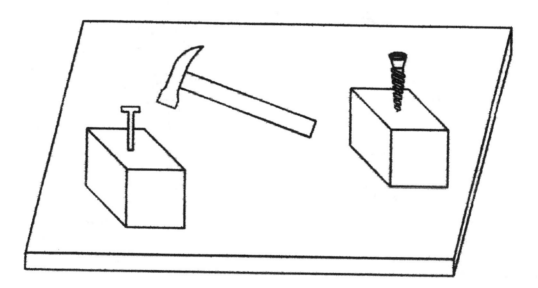

Conclusion/What is going on? In physics, a simple machine is a device that works when only a single force is applied to it. The six simple machines in physics are the inclined plane, pulley, screw, lever, wedge, and wheel and axle. The screw is an example of both a wedge and an inclined plane. It can be used as a wedge to bring the larger portion of the screw through other material. The thread that circles around the screw also forms a long, spiraled inclined plane. Screws are used to join things. They are also used to lift things. You might find screwed feet on the bottom of a refrigerator that can be raised or lowered to make the refrigerator level.

Report and Present: Write out the steps and what you saw. Explain the results using "What is going on?" above to help you. Display your experiment. Make a list of ways that screws are used in everyday life.

 From Carol Peterson, *Jump into Science: Themed Science Fairs.* Westport, CT: Teacher Ideas Press. © 2007 by Carol Peterson.

Lever

Hypothesis or Statement of Purpose: To understand how a lever and fulcrum work.

What you need:

Block of wood 1 inch by 1 inch by about 6 inches long

Thick dowel or stick about 2 feet long

A book

Test, watch, and record: Rest one book on a table on top of the stick. Try to lift the book using the stick. Next place the stick on the block of wood and place the book on top of one end of the stick. Push down on the upper end of the stick to lift the book. Record your observations as to what happened on each attempt. Move the block forward and backward from the middle of the stick and repeat the experiment. Compare the effort required and record your observations. If there is a seesaw (teeter-totter) at your school or park, go there with a friend. Try sitting on the seesaw farther and closer to the middle. Observe how the place you sit affects how much weight (force) is needed to move the seesaw up and down.

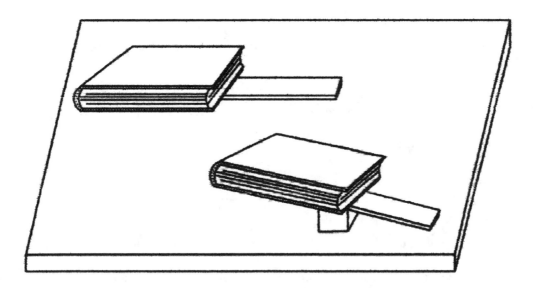

Conclusion/What is going on? In physics, a simple machine is a device that works when only a single force is applied to it. The six simple machines in physics are the inclined plane, pulley, screw, lever, wedge, and wheel and axle. A fulcrum is a point on which a lever rests. In this experiment, the stick is the lever and the block of wood is the fulcrum. You found that you were able to move the book with the lever much easier when the fulcrum was used. The location of the fulcrum along the lever affects the height you are able to lift the book.

Report and Present: Write out the steps you used in this experiment and what you saw. Explain the results using "What is going on?" above to help you. Display your book, stick, and block.

Wedge

Hypothesis or Statement of Purpose: To understand how a wedge works.

What you need:

Cardboard	Hammer
Sharpened pencil	Screw
Block of wood	Screwdriver
Nail	

Test, watch, and record: Set the cardboard on a flat surface. Push the pencil eraser down hard against the cardboard. Now turn the pencil over and press the pencil point hard against the cardboard. Record your observations. Now try to insert a screw into a block of wood using only the screw and screwdriver. Then pound a nail partly into the wood. Remove the nail. Insert a screw into the nail hole and tighten it using the screwdriver. Record your observations.

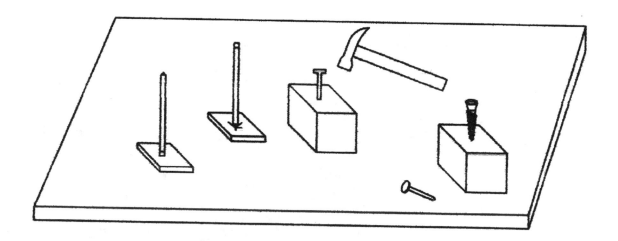

Conclusion/What is going on? In physics, a simple machine is a device that works when only a single force is applied to it. The six simple machines in physics are the inclined plane, pulley, screw, lever, wedge, and wheel and axle. The sharp point of the pencil went through at least part of the cardboard. The eraser did not go through. A wedge is an inclined plane, used to lift, pry or split another object. An inclined plane is a simple machine with an angled surface. This angle allows a small amount of force to be used over a longer distance. For example, walking up a sloped trail that zigzags back and forth is easier to hike than going straight up the side of a steep mountain. The point of the pencil acts like a wedge, pushing into the cardboard to create a path for the larger part of the pencil to follow. You should find it easier for the screw to enter the wood if you first make a small hole for it with the nail. Downward force on the wedge (by the screwdriver) produces sideways force on another object (pushing the screw through the wood).

Report and Present: Write out the steps and what you saw. Explain the results using "What is going on?" above to help you. Display your cardboard, pencil, block of wood, and screw.

Wheel and Axle (Gears)

Hypothesis or Statement of Purpose: To understand how two wheels and axles can form gears.

What you need:

> Two Styrofoam circles
>
> Toothpicks
>
> Two pencils

Note: This experiment can also be done using Tinkertoys.

Test, watch, and record: Insert six toothpicks equally into the sides of each Styrofoam circle. Insert a sharpened pencil into the center of each circle. Place one circle on a flat surface with the pencil eraser pointing up. Place the second circle next to it with the pencil horizontally, as shown. Make sure the toothpicks of the wheels intersect each other. Hold the vertical pencil loosely and turn the horizontal pencil. Observe the direction and movement of both wheels.

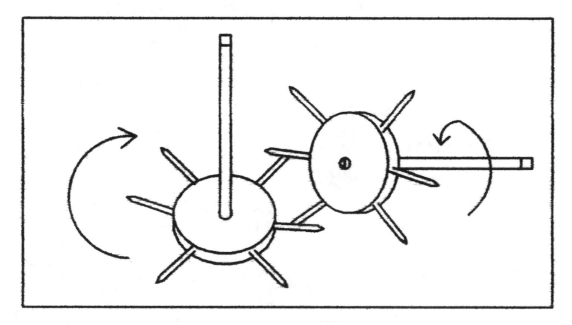

Conclusion/What is going on? In physics, a simple machine is a device that works when only a single force is applied to it. The six simple machines in physics are the inclined plane, pulley, screw, lever, wedge, and wheel and axle. The circle with the pencil in the center forms a wheel and axle. The toothpicks form gears. When the teeth of two gears fit together, the movement of one gear turns the second gear.

Report and Present: Write out the steps and what you saw. Explain the results using "What is going on?" above to help you. Bring in a kitchen eggbeater or a bicycle as an example of common gears that people use. Think about how gears are used in other areas and how they could be used in alternative energy sources.

PHYSICAL FORCES

 ## Air Resistance

Hypothesis or Statement of Purpose: To understand air resistance.

What you need:

Two feathers

Two leaves about the same size

One sheet of tissue paper

Scissors

Test, watch, and record: Fold the sheet of tissue paper in half and cut 2 pieces of paper the same size. Hold a feather in each hand away from your body—one feather with the shaft pointing to the ground and the other feather flat to the ground. Release them at the same time. Observe how they fall. Now hold a leaf in each hand away from your body—one leaf with the stem pointing to the ground and the other flat to the ground. Release them at the same time. Observe how they fall. Now scrunch one piece of tissue paper into a ball. Hold the ball in one hand and the open tissue paper in the other away from your body. Release them at the same time. Observe and record how they fall.

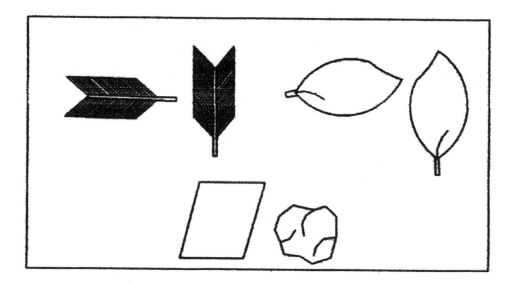

Conclusion/What is going on? Several things are going on—gravity (the force from the Earth trying to pull objects to the ground), weight, and air resistance. Gravity pulls all objects to the ground at the same rate. The weight of an object can affect its speed. Here, the objects are of similar weight. So the speed of the objects falling also has to do with how much air it has to push out of the way. The small ball of paper fell faster than the sheet. The feather and leaf pointing down had less air to push out of the way than when dropped flat and so fell faster. Think how this relates to parachutes.

Report and Present: Write out the steps and what you saw. Explain the results using "What is going on?" above to help you. Display your objects.

Bridge Engineering

Hypothesis or Statement of Purpose: To understand what type of bridge holds the most weight.

What you need:

Seven pieces of thin cardboard about 10 inches long and 4 to 6 inches wide

Strip of corrugated cardboard about 10 inches long and 4 to 6 inches wide

Two stacks of books the same height

Paper cup

Weight—sand, pebbles, or dirt

Tape

Spoon

Scissors

Pen or pencil

Ruler

Test, watch, and record: 1) Working outside, set two equal stacks of books about 6 inches from each other on a flat surface. Set one piece of thin cardboard across the books. Place the empty cup in the center of the cardboard. Add spoonfuls of weight to the cup until the bridge collapses. Record the number of spoonfuls before the bridge collapsed. Then test the following types of bridges, adding weight to the cup, one spoonful at a time. Record the number of spoonfuls before each bridge collapses or the cup is full. 2) Bend a strip of cardboard upward into an arch to create a bridge. 3) Measure, mark, and cut 2 inches off another strip of cardboard. Fold the 8-inch strip into a long triangle. Tape together. Center a flat side of the triangle to another strip of cardboard. Tape in place and set it between the books triangle point down. 4) Tape three strips of cardboard together and set between the books. 5) Place the corrugated cardboard between the books.

Conclusion/What is going on? You found that the triangular truss and the corrugated cardboard bridges were the strongest. A triangle shape supports weight by distributing stress. Tear off the top layer of the corrugated cardboard. Inside you will find triangular tubes.

Report and Present: Write out the steps and what you saw. Explain the results using "What is going on?" above to help you. Builders use triangular roof frames so that the weight of the roof is supported better. Display your data table and the cardboard pieces you used.

From Carol Peterson, *Jump into Science: Themed Science Fairs*. Westport, CT: Teacher Ideas Press. © 2007 by Carol Peterson.

Center of Gravity

Hypothesis or Statement of Purpose: To understand how to locate an object's center of gravity.

What you need:

      A potato

      Two identical metal forks

      Two plastic forks

Test, watch, and record: Try to balance the potato on the end of your finger. Record the difficulty of doing so. Push plastic forks into opposite sides of the potato, at an angle. Now try to balance the potato on your finger. Record the difficulty. Remove the plastic forks and replace them with metal forks. Now try to balance it. Record the difficulty.

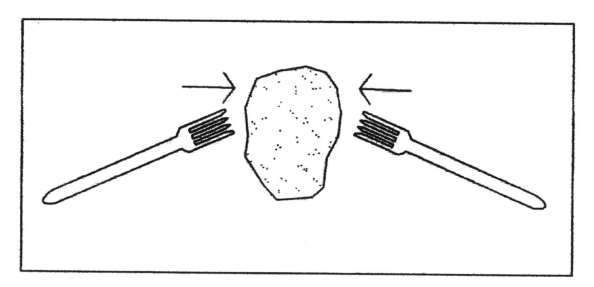

Conclusion/What is going on? Because it is difficult to locate the potato's center of gravity, you have trouble balancing it. The "mass" of the forks moves the center of gravity to a place where the potato can be balanced. But plastic forks don't have as much mass as metal forks. Therefore they don't move the potato's center of gravity enough to be balanced.

Report and Present: Write out the steps and what you saw. Explain the results using "What is going on?" above to help you. Relate this to the long pole a tightrope walker uses to lower his or her center of gravity toward the rope and stay balanced. Display this with a fresh potato.

 From Carol Peterson, *Jump into Science: Themed Science Fairs*. Westport, CT: Teacher Ideas Press.

Glider

Hypothesis or Statement of Purpose: To understand how air resistance affects flight.

What you need:

Two sheets of 8½ by 11–inch paper   Measuring tape
Small paper clip   Tape or an object to mark the ground

Test, watch, and record: Fold one sheet of paper in half lengthwise. Open the paper. Then fold each top side in toward the center line at an angle as shown. Repeat with a second, third, and fourth fold in toward the center fold on both sides. Slide a small paper clip onto the nose of the glider. Mark the ground where you stand. Hold the glider with the nose pointing forward and toss it forward. Use the measuring tape to measure the distance it flew. Record the distance. Now remove the paper clip from the glider. Standing on your mark, release the glider again. Measure and record the distance it flew.

Now take the second sheet of paper and crumple it into a loose ball. Stand on your mark and toss the ball using about the same throwing power. Measure and record the distance. Now open the crumpled ball and place the paperclip in the center. Crumple the paper into a tight ball. Stand on your mark and throw it. Measure, record, and compare all distances.

Conclusion/What is going on? There are two forces at work. Gravity pulls objects toward the ground. But air underneath the paper wings pushes up against the glider, providing resistance against the pull of gravity. The paper clip on the nose of the plane provides mass to the paper to help it move forward and to keep it going farther and longer. The crumpled ball of paper has the same mass as the glider without the paper clip; the paper that is tightly crumpled with the paperclip in the center has the same mass as the glider and paper clip.

Report and Present: Write out the steps and what you saw. Explain the results using "What is going on?" above to help you. Display your glider, ball of paper, and record of distances.

Attraction of Water

Hypothesis or Statement of Purpose: To understand how water molecules are attracted to each other.

What you need:

Large plastic disposable cup   Pitcher
Nail   Access to a sink (or do this outside on a table)
Water

Test, watch, and record: With a nail, punch four holes near the bottom of a disposable plastic cup. Try to keep the holes fairly close together and in a straight line. Set the cup on the side of a sink or on a table outside. Make sure the holes of the cup are next to the edge of the sink or table. Fill the cup with water. Observe the water as it runs out the holes. Then as the water continues to run through the holes, "pinch" the streams of water together with your fingers. Pour more water into the cup as you observe the water flow. Record your observations.

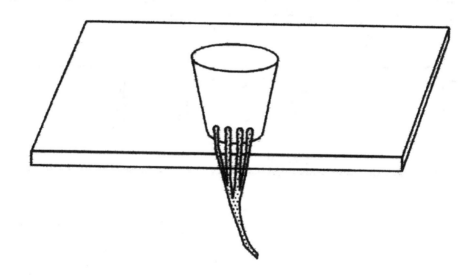

Conclusion/What is going on? At first the water comes out of the holes in four separate streams. When you "pinch" them together, they unite. Water molecules are attracted to other water molecules. The molecules will pull other molecules toward them and cause them to stick together. This attraction is also why you can fill a glass of water so that the level is slightly above the level of the glass. The molecules of water are attracted to each other and therefore keep the water from spilling over the side. Try this experiment using other liquids, such as rubbing alcohol. Remember that some liquids are made up of mostly water. How would that affect your results? Other liquids such as soda pop contain gasses. How would that affect your results?

Report and Present: Write out the steps and what you saw. Explain the results using "What is going on?" above to help you. Perform this experiment at your presentation, using a large bucket or tub to catch the water streams. Or draw pictures showing the stages of the experiment.

From Carol Peterson, *Jump into Science: Themed Science Fairs.* Westport, CT: Teacher Ideas Press. © 2007 by Carol Peterson.

Friction

Hypothesis or Statement of Purpose: To understand how rollers can counter friction.

What you need:

Two or three books	Ruler
2 feet of string	Large rubber band
Scissors	10 round pencils

Test, watch, and record: Measure the length of the rubber band. Tie a string around a book. Tie the rubber band to the string and place one or two more books on top of the first. Pull on the rubber band to move the books toward you. Stop pulling as the books begin to move but do not release the rubber band. Measure the length of the rubber band. Release and record the measurement. Now place the pencils on the table to form rollers. Place the books on top of them. Again begin to pull the rubber band. When the books begin to move, measure and record the length of the rubber band.

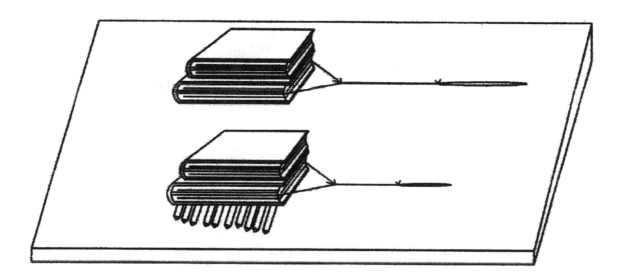

Conclusion/What is going on? The rubber band will stretch longer when pulling the books not on rollers. The sliding of the books on the table causes friction. When the books are on rollers, only a small area of each pencil is in contact with the table. Therefore there is less friction between the pencil and the table than between the large book and the table. The difference in friction is shown by the change in length of the rubber band.

Report and Present: Write out the steps you used in this experiment and what you saw. Explain the results using "What is going on?" above to help you. Display the book tied to the string and rubber band and the pencils.

Whirligig and Parachutes

Hypothesis or Statement of Purpose: To understand the relationship between lift and air resistance.

What you need:

Three paper towels	Paper plate slightly smaller than paper towel
Sheet of construction paper	Pencil
Scissors	Three small paper clips
Ruler	String

Test, watch, and record: Make a whirligig by cutting out a shape 4 inches long by 1½ inches wide. Cut along the solid lines in the first figure and fold along dotted lines. Roll the handle where shown on the dotted lines. Hold the whirligig between your hands and roll it, pushing forward with the right hand and back with the left, while releasing it into the air. Observe the whirligig's flight and landing.

Using pencil, ruler, plate, and scissors, cut a square, a triangle, and a circle out of the paper towels about 8 inches overall. Poke a hole in the corners of the square and triangle with the end of the paperclip and make 4 holes around the edge of the circle, about the same distance from each other. Cut 11 lengths of string 8 inches long. Tie one end of string to each of the holes on the paper towels. Then gather the strings on each parachute together and attach each parachute to a separate paper clip. One by one, scrunch up the parachutes and toss them into the air. Record which design is most effective at slowing the fall.

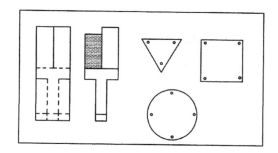

Conclusion/What is going on? Both whirligigs and parachutes show how air resistance slows their fall. The whirligig turns so that the shaft points down. As it falls, the upper flap acts like a rotor and turns to slow its landing. The air pressure below the rotors pushes up, providing upward thrust to lift the whirligig and slow its descent. A parachute only uses air resistance to slow its fall. A parachute must also allow air inside to be released so it can fall. The square parachute has the best balance of resistance and release because, as the four corners are pulled down, the open sides create four vents to allow air to escape. The triangle has less space inside compared with the outside edges. With less air resistance, it falls faster. The circular parachute has more air resistance but less stability, so it rocks back and forth during its fall. What shape parachutes do people generally use for skydiving? Why do you think that is?

Report and Present: Write out the steps and what you saw. Explain the results using "What is going on?" above to help you. Let students conduct races, guessing first which parachute will work best.

 From Carol Peterson, *Jump into Science: Themed Science Fairs.* Westport, CT: Teacher Ideas Press.
© 2007 by Carol Peterson.

Siphon

Hypothesis or Statement of Purpose: To understand how a siphon works.

What you need:

Pitcher	Clean tubing or length of garden hose
Water	Drinking glass

Test, watch, and record: Fill a pitcher with water. Place one end of a tube into it. Suck on the other end of the tube until the water reaches your lips. With your finger, cap the end of the tube without letting any air get into it. Keeping your finger on the end of the tube, place the capped end into the drinking glass. Remove your finger. The water will flow into the glass from the pitcher as long as the level of the water in the pitcher is higher. Record your observations.

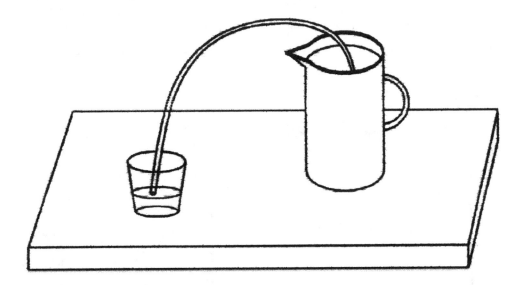

Conclusion/What is going on? This experiment is an example of a siphon pump. This pump uses the natural pressure from the higher water level inside the pitcher to flow to a lower level.

Report and Present: Write out the steps and what you saw. Explain the results using "What is going on?" above to help you. Display your siphon. Have towels ready for spills.

Centripetal Force

Hypothesis or Statement of Purpose: To understand centripetal force.

What you need:

    Eight small metal washers

    Empty spool of thread

    String, about 3 feet long

Tie one end of the string to one washer. Slide the free end of the string through the spool and securely tie the other seven washers to the bottom end of the string. Outside, hold the spool away from your body so the single washer and about 5 inches of string are on top of the spool and the seven washers hang from the bottom. Make a circular motion with your hand to start the single washer spinning in a circle. Increase the speed until the washer is going fast. Record your observations about the bottom washers.

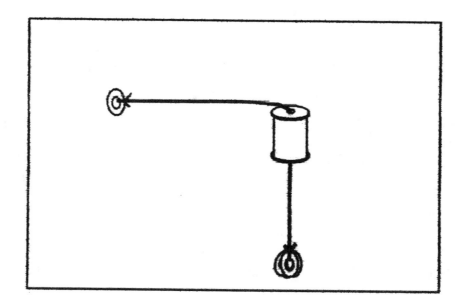

Conclusion/What is going on? Objects want to move in a straight line. As the top washer spins, it tries to fly off in a straight line. When an object goes in a circle, it is actually changing directions constantly and is being pulled toward the center of the circle. That means that the faster an object spins, the more force is needed to keep it going in a circle. The tension between the top washer's attempt to go straight as it being forced in a circle, pulls the bottom washers up.

Report and Present: Write out the steps and what you saw. Explain the results using "What is going on?" above to help you. Think about spinning rides at the fair that force you outward. Make drawings of your observations to display along with your string.

BEHAVIOR OF PHYSICAL LAWS

Electrical Current

Hypothesis or Statement of Purpose: To understand how to create a simple electrical circuit.

What you need:

12 inches of thin copper wire	Salt
6 inches of thick copper wire	Water
12 inches of insulated wire cut equally in two pieces	Pencil
	Spoon
A small Styrofoam ball	Masking tape
6-volt battery	Scissors
Small bowl	Six to eight books

Test, watch, and record: Twist thin wire around a pencil to form a coil. Slip the coil off the pencil. Push the thick wire into the bottom of the Styrofoam ball. Then push the sharp end of the pencil into the side of the ball. Lay the pencil on a stack of books with the thick wire extending from the bottom of the ball. Tape the pencil to the books. Stretch the coiled wire slightly to form a spring. Twist one end to connect it to the thick wire. With scissors, strip the plastic from both ends of the insulated wires. Attach one end of each insulated wire to one of the battery terminals. Twist the other end of one of the insulated wires to the thick wire.

Fill a bowl with warm water, adding salt and stirring until no more salt dissolves. Place the bowl so that the coil sits below the water surface, adding or removing books, if necessary. Place the loose insulated wire into the water. Now remove the spring from the water. Replace the spring into the water and remove the insulated wire. Record your observations.

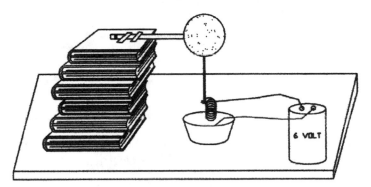

Conclusion/What is going on? The wire formed a simple electrical circuit. The electricity passing through the spring turns the spring into a magnet with a north and south pole that attract each other and pull the spring together. But as the spring tightens, the end is pulled out of the water, which breaks the circuit. Without electricity, the spring no longer acts as a magnet and stretches out again, causing it to touch the water, which recreates the circuit. An "electrolyte" is a liquid that conducts electricity. Adding salt to the water creates an electrolyte, which helps form this electrical circuit.

Report and Present: Write out the steps and what you saw. Explain the results using "What is going on?" above to help you. Demonstrate your circuit for other students.

From Carol Peterson, *Jump into Science: Themed Science Fairs*. Westport, CT: Teacher Ideas Press. © 2007 by Carol Peterson.

Simple Battery

Hypothesis or Statement of Purpose: To understand a simple circuit.

What you need:

    Lemon

    Length of copper wire (6 inches)

    Paper clip

Test, watch, and record: Unbend the paper clip and stick it into the lemon past the rind and into the juicy part of the fruit. Touch the paper clip to your tongue and record your observation. Now stick the short length of wire into the lemon near the paper clip. Touch the end of the copper wire to your tongue. Record your observations. Now touch the ends of both the paperclip and the wire to your tongue at the same time. Observe and record your observations. Other fruits and vegetables such as potatoes and pineapples that contain acid can also be used to make simple batteries. Try different ones and compare which work best.

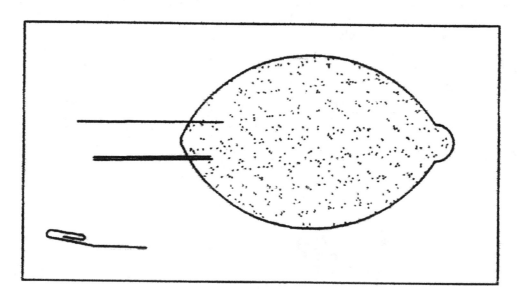

Conclusion/What is going on? The tingle on your tongue when you touch it to both wires is electricity. The two wires and the acid in the lemon form a simple electrical circuit. If you only use one of the wires, you do not have a complete circuit.

Report and Present: Write out the steps and what you saw. Explain the results using "What is going on?" above to help you. Display your battery, with a fresh lemon, if needed.

Induction

Hypothesis or Statement of Purpose: To understand induction by creating an induction coil and galvanometer.

What you need:

Bar magnet

5 feet of enameled (NOT plastic insulated) copper wire

Magnetic compass

Four twisty ties

Ruler

Scissors

Test, watch, and record: Wrap the copper wire around your hand several times, leaving about 18 inches of wire at both ends. Slide the coil off your hand and tie in place with twisty ties. Twist the two loose ends of the wire together. Wrap the loose ends in the same direction as one, around the compass. This turns the compass into a "galvanometer"—a device that determines the presence, direction, and strength of electric current.

Hold the coil in one hand. Slowly move the bar magnet in and out of the center of the coil. Observe the compass needle. Now move the bar magnet in and out of the coil quickly. Observe the compass needle and record your observations.

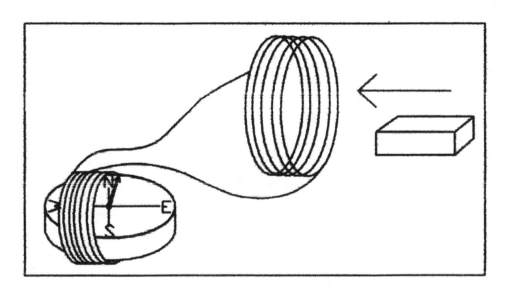

Conclusion/What is going on? The needle of the compass jumps as you move the magnet inside the coil, creating an electrical current in the wire. This current is called "induction." When you remove the magnet, the current is stopped. Moving the magnet quickly creates a pulse of electrical current. This pulsing current is called "alternating current," referred to as "AC," and is the most common type of electricity used.

Report and Present: Write out the steps and what you saw. Explain the results using "What is going on?" above to help you. Display your galvanometer.

Static Electricity

Hypothesis or Statement of Purpose: To understand static electricity.

What you need:

Plastic comb	Scissors
Aluminum foil	Balloon

Test, watch, and record: With the scissors, cut 10 or 12 tiny pieces of foil about ¼ inch square. Lay the foil pieces on a table. Run the comb through your hair several times and then hold the comb near—but not touching—the foil pieces. Record your observations. Then blow up a balloon and tie the end. Rub the balloon against your hair. Then hold the balloon close to a wall and release the balloon.

Conclusion/What is going on? Under normal conditions, an object has the same number of positively charged protons and negatively charged electrons. That makes the object electrically neutral. Electrons, however, can move about while protons remain stationary. Therefore when you run the comb through your hair, it rubs electrons off your hair and onto the comb. When the comb is then held against the foil, the neutral protons are attracted to the comb, causing the foil to jump toward the comb. After the negative electrons on the comb pass onto the foil, they have negative charges that repel each other, causing the foil to jump away from the comb. Rubbing the balloon brushes electrons onto your hair, giving each hair the same type of charge. Hair can't get rid of any extra charge, so the hairs repel each other, making them stand up. Like charges repel from each other. Unlike charges attract each other. The balloon contained charged electrons. So did the wall. Therefore they attracted each other.

Report and Present: Write out the steps you used and what you saw. Explain the results using "What is going on?" above to help you. Have extra balloons for students to try the experiments themselves.

Jet Engines

Hypothesis or Statement of Purpose: To understand how jet engines operate.

What you need:

Plastic tray from microwave food	Scissors
Plastic straw	Large tub or sink
Modeling clay	Water
Balloon	Sharp nail
Tape	

Test, watch, and record: Blow up the balloon to stretch it. Let out the air. Stick the end of the straw inside the opening of the balloon and tape the balloon end securely to the straw so that it is airtight. Make a hole at one end of tray with a sharp nail. Enlarge the hole with the point of the scissors and insert the straw through hole, as shown. Blow up the balloon and seal the straw with a small amount of clay. Set the boat in water at one end of a tub with the straw toward the wall of the tub. Release the boat and snip off the clay end of the straw. Record your observations.

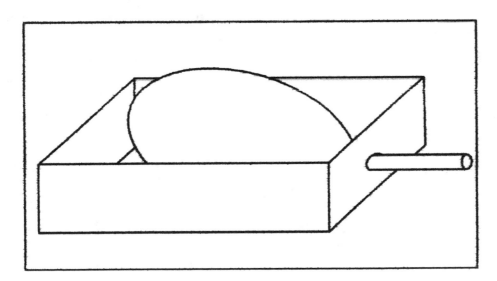

Conclusion/What is going on? When the end of the straw is clipped, the air in the balloon pushes its way through the straw. This air release pushes the boat forward. Jet engines and rockets work the same way, propelling the aircraft forward by pushing gas out the back. In addition to pushing gas, designers also use principles of air pressure, lift, and momentum to keep the aircraft moving up and forward.

Report and Present: Write out the steps and what you saw. Explain the results using "What is going on?" above to help you. Draw diagrams and display them and your boat.

Reflection

Hypothesis or Statement of Purpose: To understand reflection.

What you need:

Sheet of white paper	Flashlight
Sheet of black paper	Dark room or closet
Sheet of red paper	Masking tape

Test, watch, and record: Tape the sheets of paper next to each other on a wall in a dark room or closet. Turn out the lights and shine the flashlight on the white paper. Then shine the flashlight on the black paper. Then shine it on the red paper. Turn on the light and record your observations.

Conclusion/What is going on? The reflection of light on white paper is a full circle of bright light. The reflection on black paper is less light because the black paper absorbs the light rather than reflecting it. The light reflected on the red paper is red. White light is made up of many colors. This shows that the red paper reflects back only the red light within the color spectrum.

Report and Present: Write out the steps and what you saw. Explain the results using "What is going on?" above to help you.

 From Carol Peterson, *Jump into Science: Themed Science Fairs.* Westport, CT: Teacher Ideas Press. © 2007 by Carol Peterson.

Spectrum of Light

Hypothesis or Statement of Purpose: To understand the spectrum of colors in white light.

What you need:

Flashlight

Mirror with straight sides (about 6
    inches long)

Cake pan

Water

Sheet of white paper

Masking tape

Modeling clay

Pitcher

Test, watch, and record: Place a table next to a wall. Set a cake pan on the table. Tape the sheet of white paper on the wall above the pan. Place a lump of clay on the bottom of the pan near the edge across from the paper. Rest the mirror between the clay and the edge of the pan so that the mirror stands at a 45-degree angle (halfway between standing straight up and lying down), with the mirror side pointing to the paper. Using the pitcher, fill the pan with water. Shine the flashlight onto the water so the light shines through the water, onto the mirror, and then reflects off the mirror onto the paper. Then shine the flashlight directly onto the mirror, shine it at different angles, and change the angle of the mirror. Record your observations.

Conclusion/What is going on? We see white light. White light is actually made of many colors. This experiment refracts (breaks up) this light. Once broken up, the colors spread out to form a spectrum (lengths of the light waves) that we can see on the paper.

Report and Present: Write out the steps and what you saw. Explain the results using "What is going on?" above to help you. Display the pieces of your experiment.

Frequency of Sound

Hypothesis or Statement of Purpose: To understand how sound waves travel at different speeds.

What you need:

       Two tops from shoeboxes

       Two sets of rubber bands in various sizes

Test, watch, and record: Organize your rubber bands according to thickness. Place them around the box top, spaced apart, with the thinnest rubber bands on one end and the thickest at the other end. Now place the second set of rubber bands on the second box top in the same order, but lengthwise. Pluck the narrowest rubber band and note the pitch. Pluck another band and note its pitch. Does it sound higher or lower than the first? Compare the thinnest rubber bands on both box tops and the thickest. Repeat with all rubber bands, and record your observations. Pluck the first rubber band and then gently touch it with your finger. Now pluck the last rubber band and touch it with your finger. Which of the rubber bands felt like it was vibrating faster?

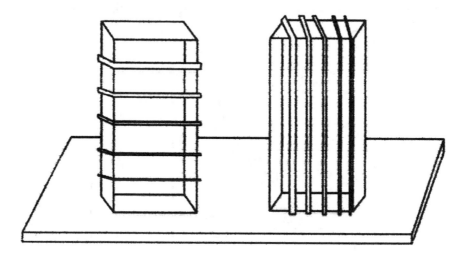

Conclusion/What is going on? Stretching the rubber bands makes them narrower. The narrower rubber bands should make a sound that is a higher pitch. Also the narrower rubber bands vibrate faster. Music is made by different sounds. Different pitches of sound (higher and lower) are made by waves that vibrate differently and at different frequencies (either faster or slower). Musical instruments vibrate sound in different ways. Percussion instruments such as drums and pianos produce sound when they are hit. Stringed instruments produce sound when their strings are plucked or moved with a bow. Wind instruments produce sound when the air inside them vibrates. Which type of instrument best describes the box top?

Report and Present: Write out the steps and what you saw. Explain the results using "What is going on?" above to help you. Display your box tops and have photos of various musical instruments labeled with how that type of instrument creates sound.

Seeing Sound Waves

Hypothesis or Statement of Purpose: To understand sound waves by seeing them visually.

What you need:

Straight-sided metal bowl or empty cookie tin

Plastic wrap

Large rubber band

Salt

Metal pan

Spoon

Five identical soda bottles filled with different amounts of water

Test, watch, and record: Cover a straight-sided metal bowl or empty cookie tin with plastic wrap. Hold the plastic in place with a large rubber band. Pour a spoon of salt onto the plastic. Bang a metal pan near the cookie tin. Bang softly, quickly, and slowly. Observe the salt and record your observations. Then set the bottles on a table. Blow across the openings to vibrate the air inside. Which bottle makes the highest sound; the lowest?

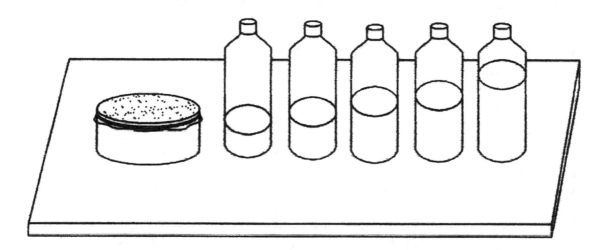

Conclusion/What is going on? Sound travels through the air in waves. These waves hit the plastic wrap and make it vibrate which causes the salt to dance in time to the sound made by the spoon. The closer together the sound waves flow, the higher sound they make. Therefore the less air in the bottle (the more water), the higher the pitch.

Report and Present: Write out the steps and what you saw. Explain the results using "What is going on?" above to help you. Display your plastic covered cookie tin and bottles.

Hypothesis or Statement of Purpose: To understand how sound can be made by shock waves instead of vibrations.

What you need:

Sheet of copy paper

Test, watch, and record: Fold a sheet of paper in half lengthwise. Open the paper and fold each corner in toward the fold. Refold at the center lengthwise. Now fold the paper in half to form a triangle with one point cut off. Fold the top point down even with the bottom edge and covering the cut-off side. Turn over and repeat the last step. You should end with a triangle. Open the middle pouch.

Hold the triangle at the two long points between your thumb and middle finger with your index finger inside the pouch—open end away from you. Make sure you also grasp the back half of the pouch fold, leaving the front half free. Poke the pouch back inside the triangle so the front half of the fold is in front of your index finger. Turn your hand over so that your palm faces the floor. Lift your hand over your head and swing it down quickly. When you stop, the paper folded inside will swing out, causing a bang.

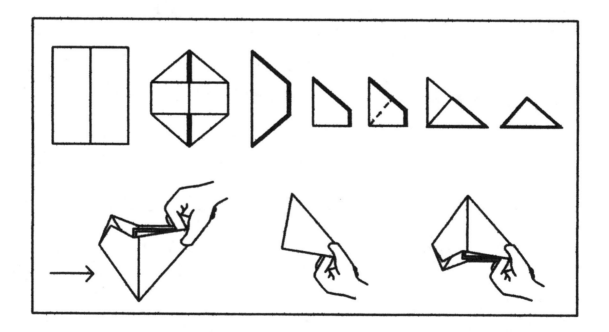

Conclusion/What is going on? Most sounds are produced by vibrations in the air when an object moves through it. But some sounds, such as shock waves, are made by sudden air movements when an object moves quickly. An example of a sound from a shock wave is the sound made by a bullet fired from a gun.

Report and Present: Write out the steps and what you saw. Explain the results using "What is going on?" above to help you. Demonstrate your noisemaker.

Appendix:
Tips for Students

Planning: Read through the "Safety Rules," "The Scientific Method," and your chosen experiment's instructions before you conduct your experiment. Gather your instructions, items listed in the experiment, paper and pencil to record steps taken and observations or results, and a camera or paper and pencil for drawing important observations. Make sure you know how much time your experiment will take because you may need several days or weeks to complete it.

Experiment: Stop, observe, and record often during your experiment. That will give you a clear idea what is happening and make it easier for you to prepare your report. If you have time, repeat the experiment to verify results. Don't rush. Spend time on the project.

Report and Presentation: Scientific discovery is shared so everyone can learn. In your report, state the problem clearly. Define the variables and controls you used. Create tables, graphs, and illustrations to interpret data. Do extra research if needed to help you understand the data. Collect enough data to make a conclusion. Justify your conclusion based on data collected in the experiment. Summarize what you learned. Use the display during your presentation to help others understand. Practice your presentation out loud and in front of other people. Point out things in your display during your presentation.

Create an interesting display that will attract others. Use a colored cloth to cover your table and place graphs, charts, reports, and drawings on colored papers for visual appeal. Create a three-sided display of cardboard or foam board about 48 inches wide, 30 inches deep, and 108 inches high, including the table the board stands on. You can buy displays at most office supply stores. Or you can make one by dividing a large sheet of cardboard lengthwise into three sections and carefully slicing *part way* through one side of the cardboard so it can be bent.

Include the title of your project at the top of the middle section of the board. The title should be 6 to 10 words and large enough to be read easily from 3 feet away. Try not to put too much information on your display, but place parts of it (the report, for example) on the table underneath. Include a short summary of the project in 100 words or less. Use headings such as "Problem," "Procedure," "Results," and "Conclusion," or other titles that help explain your project in a way that is easy for people to see and understand.

The Scientific Method

FIRST, State the problem or question. Try to ask questions that begin with "how does," "why do," or "what makes?" Problems should need to be answered by experimenting.

SECOND, Form a Hypothesis. This is a statement about what you think is the answer. The hypothesis should state one or more facts you will test to prove, disprove, or explain your idea. Include facts that might affect your hypothesis. Write the hypothesis before you start testing. Not all experiments require a hypothesis. Some experiments are just a way to understand a scientific concept.

THIRD, Experimentation. This is a controlled observation to test your hypothesis. Each experiment will have things that effect what is happening, called "variables." An **independent variable** is something you change on purpose to see how it affects the result. A **dependent variable** is what happens in response to the independent variable. A **controlled variable** is something that does not change each time the experiment is performed. Make sure to have only one independent variable each time so you can see what is affecting your results. Try also to have a control so you can compare each experiment. If you have time, repeat the experiment to check your results. Keep a record of what you do, what you observe, and your results.

FOURTH, Conclusion. This is a summary of the results of your experiment. It also includes a statement of how the results compare to your hypothesis. When writing your conclusion, don't change your hypothesis based on the results or leave out any results even if they don't support your hypothesis. If results are different from your hypothesis, give possible reasons why and think of ways you might change the process of your experiment or do further testing.

FIFTH, Report. This final step is to share your results with other people so that they can learn, too. This reporting is what you will do during your presentation.

Student Safety Rules

- Work in an area that has enough space and fresh air.

- Cover your work area with newspaper or plastic, if needed. Clean up spills right away.

- If needed, wear an apron, goggles, gloves, or a facemask and use tongs and hot pads when necessary.

- Have an adult help you when using sharp knives and stoves or ovens.

- Never taste or smell chemicals; avoid chemical contact with skin and eyes. Label all containers used in your experiment that hold chemicals.

- Do not go on a field trip alone. Tell an adult where you are going, how you plan to get there, and how long you will be. Stick with your plan. Dress for where you are going, including the right shoes. Check the list of items needed to make sure you take everything you will need. Plan how you will bring large, bulky or messy items back with you.

Tips for Teachers

Here are some ideas to use this resource creatively:

Conduct a classroom science fair as a whole- or half-day event.

Have a science fair to begin or end a classroom study for that area of science to generate more interest and enthusiasm.

Turn the event into a classroom party.

Have a science fair at the end of the year on the date of an open house so parents can also enjoy the displays.

Invite lower-grade classes to observe the presentations.

Use individual experiments in class to teach specific areas of science.

Use the cross-referencing icons to locate other experiments that can be used for specific areas of science.

Reproduce the award certificate provided on the next page. Grant one award for best in show, or grant an award to each student, using creative or funny categories, such as "most detailed," "best visuals," "best oral presentation," "best written report," "gooiest project," "neatest display."

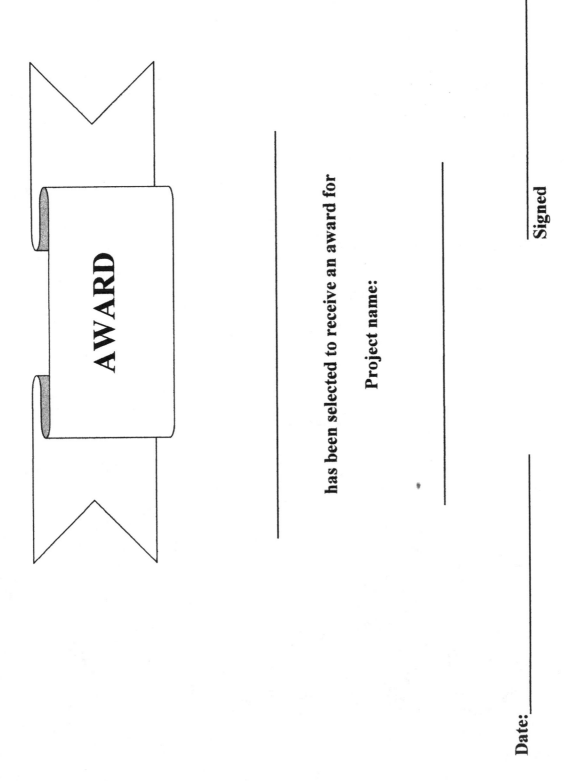

AWARD

has been selected to receive an award for

Project name:

Signed

Date:

Bibliography

Bazler, Judith A., Ed. D. *Science Experiments on File*. New York: Facts on File, 2000.

Burnie, David. *How Nature Works*. London: Reader's Digest, 1991.

Cutnell, John D., and Kenneth W. Johnson. *Physics*. New York: John Wiley & Sons, 1998.

Graham, John, Peter Mellett, Jack Challoner, and Sarah Angliss. Illustrated by David Le Jars. *Hands-on Science*. New York: Kingfisher, 2001.

Tanacredi, John T. *Experiment Central*. (4 volumes). Item ID 4535761. Detroit, MI: Thompson Gale.

Wood, Robert W. *Physics for Kids*. Blue Ridge Summit, PA: Tab Books, 1990.

Index

About the Author

"Make learning fun" is Carol's theme. She combines a love of the world around her with a passion for instilling in children a joy of learning by creating fun, hands-on activities for kids. Carol holds a multi-departmental degree from the University of California at Davis, which combined history, geography, sociology, economics, and political science. Over the past fifteen years, thousands of children have enjoyed the educational activities she has developed for schools, scouting groups, and children's charities.